MW01028218

PRAISE FOR STEVE FARBER AND
LOVE IS JUST DAMN GOOD BUSINESS

We live in a world that's yearning for unity and purpose in work, but finding it can seem impossible. The answer? Love. Steve Farber makes a clear case that "operationalizing" love as the core principle of your business will bring people together and produce powerful results.

> —JACK CANFIELD, coauthor of the *Chicken Soup for the Soul®* series and *The Success Principles™: How to Get from Where You Are to Where You Want to Be*

Love is the most powerful force in the world. Steve Farber captures this in his book as a relevant and necessary act of doing business and being in the service of others. Good begets good. Well done!

> —STEDMAN GRAHAM, speaker, entrepreneur, and author of *Identity Leadership*

We all know what good business isn't. It isn't working your teams to death. Or prioritizing profits above all else. Or clueless hiring and ruthless firing. And it's no longer enough to be liked, or respected, or even trusted. To succeed in any crowded and distracted market, you must be *loved* by customers and employees alike. How? Steve Farber reveals the fascinating answers. I love this book.

> —SALLY HOGSHEAD, CEO of Fascinate® and *New York Times* bestselling author of *How the World Sees You* and *Fascinate*

They don't teach this stuff in business school, but they should! *Love Is Just Damn Good Business* is a message every leader at every level of every organization needs to take to heart and put into action. It's what I strive to do every day in my business.

—IVAN MISNER, PhD, founder of BNI and *New York Times* bestselling author of *Truth or Delusion?*

I've seen how love works in my own aptly named business, and I know it will work in yours. Thanks to Steve Farber, you now have a road map to show you the way. A book on this subject could easily have been all soft platitudes; instead, it is a serious book with pages of substantive insight and actionable advice. Read it and lead from the heart.

—ADAM MARKEL, founder of More Love Media and bestselling author of *Pivot*

If you use the perspectives, tools, and techniques in this book to build a culture centered around love, you'll rally your team and turbocharge your company—as we've done with ours. It's a phenomenal book. Don't miss it.

—KEN AND KERRI COURTRIGHT, cofounders of Income Store (a five-time Inc. 5000 company)

Too many leaders have bought into the myth that business should be cutthroat and heartless. Steve Farber upends that long-held belief by showing that love is the secret to creating a valuable, sustainable enterprise in the twenty-first century, and he proves it with his latest and, I think, greatest book.

—PHIL TOWN, investor, speaker, and *New York Times* bestselling author of *Rule #1* and *Payback Time*

I'm in love with Steve Farber's newest book! My motto for 20 years has always been "Relationships first; business second." It's truly music to my ears that love is becoming more mainstream and acceptable in the workplace, and Steve's work is blazing the trail for so many business leaders. If you've been looking for that missing ingredient to help take your success to the next level, you must read this book.

—MARI SMITH, author of *The New Relationship Marketing*

Can leaders really apply love as a profitable business principle? Absolutely! Steve Farber has studied, refined, lived, and *proven* that approach for decades. This book shows how and why it's the perfect approach in today's business world.

—DAVID M. CORBIN, president of GBK Productions and author of *Illuminate*

This book is for managers, leaders, and anyone in business who is motivated to accomplish big goals. The examples Steve provides are 100 percent authentic, undeniable, and proven. They underscore that love is more than just a nice idea—it's the foundation companies need to be successful.

—FROM THE FOREWORD BY BURTON GOLDFIELD, CEO of TriNet

LOVE IS JUST
DAMN
GOOD
BUSINESS

LOVE IS JUST DAMN

Do What You Love

GOOD

in the Service of People

BUSINESS

Who Love What You Do

STEVE FARBER

NEW YORK   CHICAGO   SAN FRANCISCO   ATHENS
LONDON   MADRID   MEXICO CITY   MILAN
NEW DELHI   SINGAPORE   SYDNEY   TORONTO

1 2 3 4 5 6 7 8 9   LCR   24 23 22 21 20 19

ISBN: 978-1-260-44122-2
MHID: 1-260-44122-9

e-ISBN: 978-1-260-44123-9
e-MHID: 1-260-44123-7

Design by Mauna Eichner and Lee Fukui

This publication is designed to provide accurate and authoritative information in regard to the subject matter covered. It is sold with the understanding that neither the author nor the publisher is engaged in rendering legal, accounting, securities trading, or other professional services. If legal advice or other expert assistance is required, the services of a competent professional person should be sought.
—*From a Declaration of Principles Jointly Adopted by a Committee of the*
American Bar Association and a Committee of Publishers and Associations

Library of Congress Cataloging-in-Publication Data

Names: Farber, Steve.
Title: Love is just damn good business : do what you love in the service of
   people who love what you do / Steve Farber.
Description: 1 Edition. | New York : McGraw-Hill Education, 2019.
Identifiers: LCCN 2019012600 (print) | LCCN 2019015567 (ebook) | ISBN
   9781260441239 () | ISBN 1260441237 () | ISBN 9781260441222 (hardback) |
   ISBN 1260441229
Subjects: LCSH: Leadership. | Love. | BISAC: BUSINESS & ECONOMICS /
   Leadership.
Classification: LCC HD57.7 (ebook) | LCC HD57.7 .F3633 2019 (print) | DDC
   650.1—dc23
LC record available at https://lccn.loc.gov/2019012600

To my late brother, Bill Farber.

He was always my biggest fan.

I'd like to think he still is.

CONTENTS

FOREWORD

M y friend Steve Farber will tell you that when love and business are combined, the results are just "damn good."

I completely agree and have seen this principle in action. As the CEO of TriNet, a $3.5 billion, publicly traded company that provides human resources expertise to thousands of small and medium-sized businesses across the United States, I can relate to everything Steve so passionately discusses in this book.

In my experience, love is a difference-maker. It brings an authenticity to a company's culture and makes leaders more human—and more effective. The right mix of love and business directly translates into how customers feel when buying our goods and services—they feel valued, and, in turn, they are loyal.

I love the influence I can have on my team of more than 3,000 employees and investors who believe in me—and the positive impact we collectively have on our valued clients. As CEO, it is my personal responsibility to ensure that the entire TriNet team is aligned and working together toward our goals and objectives. Motivating people is a critical part of being a leader—everyone wants to feel that they are part of something—and Steve's methods perfectly demonstrate how to cultivate love and allow every individual in the company to see his or her part in the bigger picture.

When I first met Steve, there was an immediate connection because of his wisdom, authenticity, and exuberant passion to improve people's lives. At the time, he had just published *The Radical Leap*, and I fell in love with the concepts in that book. Now, in

Love Is Just Damn Good Business, Steve puts the construct of love in a business context into a consumable, measurable, and verifiable method that will help companies grow and succeed.

This book is for managers, leaders, and anyone in business who is motivated to accomplish big goals. The examples Steve provides are 100 percent authentic, undeniable, and proven. They underscore that love is more than just a nice idea—it's the foundation companies need to be successful.

Love really *is* good business, and Steve has laid out a clear and important road map for how to translate love into success for your business and your career. I look forward to seeing what he does in the next chapter of his leadership journey—and I have no doubt, whatever the result, I will love it.

Burton M. Goldfield
CEO of TriNet

PREFACE:
HOW I CAME TO DO
WHAT I LOVE

There was a time in my adulthood when I wasn't doing what I loved. Like all too many people on this planet, I spent years floundering through life with no particular sense of direction or purpose—or at least not one that would enable me to support a family.

When I was a younger man, I knew exactly what I wanted to do. I had been playing guitar since I was 13, and if you had asked me in my late teens and early twenties what I was going to do with my life, my answer would have been obvious: play music, write songs, and perform.

I got married at 23, and that marriage came with a huge bonus—my first child, Angelica. By the time I was 24, my son, Saul, had joined the clan, and at that point I discovered that being a musician and—how do I put this?—*feeding people* were mutually exclusive ideas. Like a gunslinger hanging up his revolver, I hung up my guitar, and I started trying to provide for and raise a family.

That's when I got into business and eventually came to discover that I was an entrepreneur. Giving up music, however, was extraordinarily painful. I felt like I was grieving the death of a dream. Music had been such a huge part of my personality. It was part of the way I had connected with people and shared who I was. It was what I loved to do. Giving it up as a professional pursuit was so painful that I just stopped playing altogether.

At the same time, however, I began to pursue a new deeply fulfilling dream: fatherhood. I loved my family. I loved my kids. And I got deep gratification in bringing home the paycheck on the all-too-occasional times when that happened.

My first "real" job was in the commodities futures business. It was a straight commission gig, so it was feast or famine. That taught me a lot about entrepreneurship because it was really up to me to keep my boat afloat—a lesson that has served me well ever since. Discovering and growing into my natural entrepreneurial inclinations, I soon opened my own brokerage shop, which meant I paid myself a salary but only if the company created the income to allow it.

That was my baptism of fire into the world of business. It's where I learned about hiring people and motivating them to be productive, about marketing, about the stress and pressure of having to make payroll when other people are depending on you for the money to feed their families, and all of the various and sundry things every entrepreneur has to learn. I learned very quickly. And painfully.

Ironically, the main thing I learned was that even though I loved the game of business, I hated *that* business. From the outside, it looked pretty cool—the classic American Dream. I had my own company and great employees. I was my own boss. I had kids, a house, a car, a dog, and all the middle-class trappings anyone could hope for. The problem was that commodity futures is a very speculative investment, so our clients lost their money left and right. This led me to have a moral dilemma with my own business, and I just flat-out hated it.

It's one thing to have your own business; it's quite another to despise it.

So to recap, in a very short span of time, I got married and had kids (which raised the stakes in terms of responsibility as a provider), I gave up music (which caused me grief), and I got into a business that I hated. There was no music. There was no joy in going to work. And this was all before I was 30 years old.

Then came a series of pivotal moments in late 1988, early 1989. My growing family and I were still living in the Midwest (by then my younger son, Jeremy, had arrived, so I had three kids). My business partner had welched on a $25,000 funding commitment, and, consequently, my business went down in flames. I was offered and accepted a job across the country in exciting San Francisco, but it was in the same industry, which, of course, I still hated. This was someone else's company, however, so the task of making payroll fell on his shoulders, not mine. For me, it was a new chapter in a new setting and a chance to start over. Sort of.

On my lunch break one day, I found myself walking around the Financial District of beautiful downtown San Francisco. And even though I felt the excitement and promise of the place and the opportunities it represented, I was still totally, utterly, unequivocally miserable in the grueling, soulless work that I was continuing to grind out every week.

I knew two things with equal, crystal clarity: one, I had no doubt that there was something I was supposed to be doing on this planet, and, two, I had absolutely no blasted idea what it was.

Although I have a strong affinity for the spiritual, I'm not a particularly religious person. But while walking down the street on that blustery San Francisco day in 1989, feeling the woeful churn of a sailor lost at sea, I literally looked up to the sky and whispered through clenched teeth, "C'mon! Just tell me what I'm supposed to be doing, and I will gladly do it."

That was, in retrospect, a pivotal moment. I had acknowledged that longing voice in my heart that says, "I have purpose."

It might have been days, at most a few weeks later, but I soon found myself having a conversation with an old friend whom I hadn't talked to in a while. He mentioned that a mutual friend of ours was "teaching some kind of workshops for corporations." That was all he said. No more detail, no explanation.

And right then, in that moment, after hearing those few ambiguous words, all of my lights went on.

"That's it," I said. "That's what I'm supposed to be doing."

I had no idea what that was, but I knew it was for me.

I started talking to people about this "corporate training stuff," and I soon discovered that there was a whole industry out there. I had no idea there was such a thing as "training and development." I dove headlong into the research to learn who did what. That line of work, I realized, would give me the opportunity to combine my business experience with my love for working with people, and it would also allow me to make use of the performance skills I'd learned onstage.

I asked everyone I knew for leads into the industry. I created a résumé that made the case for why, inexperienced as I was, I would make a great "trainer."

I was hired by a small consulting company to do contract work teaching business writing workshops, and after I conducted my first session, I slapped "professional trainer" on my résumé. I was soon brought on board by an international training and consulting company, which gave me broad experience working with a wide variety of businesses and industries in various parts of the world. A few years later, in 1994, at the ripe old age of 36, I was hired by the famous management guru Tom Peters, and I met my mentors Jim Kouzes and Terry Pearce. As a vice president in Tom's company,

I learned about leadership at a very deep level and worked with senior executive teams across the business spectrum.

And guess what?

I loved this work; I had found my purpose.

Over the years in my time at the Tom Peters Company, my experiences in the trenches with clients, as well as my immersion into the collective bodies of work of Tom, Jim, and Terry, helped me develop my own point of view, my own leadership voice.

And there was one strong, unwavering, unrelenting conclusion that I came back to again and again: my personal quest to find meaningful work that I love to do was not unique. Nor was it arbitrary. It was, in fact, a crucial, universal principle: love is the core of great leadership, and it's at the foundation of any thriving, competitive business.

I left the Tom Peters Company in 2000, and published my first book, *The Radical Leap*, in 2004. *Leap* was followed by *The Radical Edge* and then *Greater Than Yourself*.

Now, in my early sixties, having traveled the globe to work with and speak to tens of thousands of people over the years, I can wholeheartedly say that I'm doing what I love in the service of people who love what I do.

The insidious idea that we have to sacrifice one part of ourselves to nurture another is false. Our ideal state is to be successful in our business ventures, to amplify personal joy and meaning in our lives, and to change the world for the better—all at the same time. These are not mutually exclusive ideas.

You don't have to be a jerk to make money. You don't have to sacrifice money for joy. And you don't have to be a martyr to change the world.

Love it all—that's where your success as a human being will come from.

My advice to you is this: Be totally unapologetic for the money you're earning. Be totally unapologetic for the joy you're experiencing. Be totally unapologetic for the impact you're making on the world for the better. But aspire to do all of them.

That's what we're built to do in, my opinion. And that's at the very heart of why I believe *Love Is Just Damn Good Business*. Because love is the secret sauce that makes it all possible.

I wrote this book so we could explore that together in a way that's different from my previous books. Those were works of fiction, business parables based on my experiences. This one is nonfiction, and it's filled with stories from my personal experiences, case studies and illustrations based on research and interviews, and practical advice from all sorts of leaders and their organizations. They paint a picture of why love is just damn good business and how to make it damn good for your business.

But here's where I suggest you start as you join me on this journey: Ask the questions that matter to you. Listen for the answers. And then do what you love in the service of people who love what you do.

I hope this book will serve you well in that endeavor.

ACKNOWLEDGMENTS

The early twentieth-century writer Gene Fowler famously said, "Writing is easy. All you do is stare at a blank sheet of paper until drops of blood form on your forehead." Here in the twenty-first century, we typically stare at a screen instead of paper, but it doesn't change the dynamics. Not for me, anyway. This book, however, was less of a struggle to create than my previous three, and the process resulted in less blood lost because it was not a lonely, solo venture. Far from it. Consequently, I have many people to thank.

First and foremost, my deep gratitude goes to Stephen Caldwell, my de facto coauthor, writing partner, and coconspirator in this project, for his superb way with words and his ability to represent my natural voice in his vast contributions to this enterprise. This book simply would not have been written without him. At least not in this century.

Many thanks and, of course, lots of love to the people who granted me their time, talent, wisdom, and encouragement during the process of bringing this book to life—many of whom you'll read about in the following pages: Ethan Agarwal, founder and CEO of Aaptiv; John Ballentine, cofounder of Tango Press; John Beeder, retired president and CEO of American Greetings; Werner Berger, wise sage and mountain climber; Indie Bollman, director of human resources and corporate development at Trailer Bridge; Elay Cohen, CEO and cofounder of SalesHood; Lonnie Golden, professor of economics and labor studies at Penn State University; Jill Lublin, author and PR consultant; Mitch Luciano, president and CEO of Trailer Bridge; Shawn Mahoney, managing principal at OAC; Mary Miller, CEO of JANCOA; Ivan Misner, founder of BNI; Elise Mitchell, CEO of Dentsu Aegis Public Relations Network; Dick Nettell, former SVP at Bank of America; Bryon Stephens, cofounder of Pivotal Growth Partners; Bernie Swain, cofounder of Washington Speakers Bureau; and Chris Van Gorder, president and CEO of Scripps Health. They're all rock stars for sharing their stories and vast business knowledge with me.

Love and thunderous applause to Jenna Lynch, the president of the Extreme Leadership Institute, for her preternatural positivity and uncanny ability to elevate companies to "Best Place to Work" status by operationalizing love as a business practice.

And speaking of the Extreme Leadership Institute, I pay homage to the original gang of 10 who gathered with me in San Diego to brainstorm the expansion of the organization: Bryon Stephens (again!), Ken Switzer, Karen Thrall, Timothy Johnson, Richard Corder, Jenna Lynch (again!), Indie Bollman (again!), Jason Gottlieb, Tom Nichols, and Debra Lawson. They demonstrated what genuine, love-inspired commitment looks like in business ideation. My own business, in this case.

I offer a heartfelt salute to Laura Johnstone for her clear thinking and creativity in managing the messages and content pouring out of our team. That is no small undertaking.

Eternal gratitude to the eternally wonderful Dianne Kenny, my longtime friend, colleague, personal cheerleader, and master facilitator of the The Extreme Leadership Workshop.

Thanks also to my agent, Bill Gladstone of Waterside Productions, and Casey Ebro, my editor at McGraw-Hill, for believing in me and in the importance of spreading the message of this book.

Burton Goldfield, president and CEO of TriNet, has been one of my greatest cheerleaders and advocates since he first read *The Radical Leap* many years ago, so I'm thrilled beyond measure for his contribution of the foreword to my latest missive. He's also the walking, talking, living, breathing proof that love really is just damn good business.

My inspiring collection of kids and steppies—Angelica, Saul, Jeremy, Kelsey, Heather, and Presley—have all turned out to be very fine adult human beings, and even though they've all flown the proverbial coop, they bring me great joy and inspiration every day of my life.

And finally, to Veronica—my wife, business partner, companion, best friend, and closest advisor—I have no words that will even begin to touch the depth and breadth of my love and gratitude for her presence in my life.

Maybe if I stare at the screen just a little bit longer . . .

1

LOVE IS A HARD-CORE BUSINESS PRINCIPLE. DEAL WITH IT.

Love anything, and your heart will be certainly wrung and possibly be broken. If you want to make sure of keeping it intact, you must give your heart to no one, not even to an animal. Wrap it carefully round with hobbies and little luxuries; avoid all entanglements; lock it up safe in the casket or coffin of your selfishness.
—C. S. Lewis

IN SEARCH OF GOOD BUSINESS

It's time to toss aside the touchy-feely notions of love in business and recognize the real power it holds. Love is not only appropriate in the context of business. It's also the foundation of great leadership, and, therefore, it's the very foundation of a thriving, competitive enterprise.

Now, you won't find too many leaders who say they are antilove. It's like saying you are antifun or antichildren or antihappiness or anti–apple pie. It's just not good for your personal brand

1

to allow such words to pass your lips. But you don't have to look far to find leaders who—by their actions, if not by their words—don't believe love should have a chair at the boardroom tables of business. If you sit in on a board of directors meeting or an executive strategy planning session or just about any other high-level leadership gathering, the last word you're likely to hear is *love*, even among those leaders who are sincerely motivated by it.

Poets write about love. Musicians sing about love. Clergy preach about love. Business leaders? They talk about profits, market share, growth potential, innovation, sales data, return on investment, competitive analysis—you know . . . business stuff. And it's all vitally important. But here's what I'm telling you: Love isn't just a concept for the "soft side" of leadership. Love, my friends, is just damn good business.

What, exactly, is "good business," you ask? To find out, I turned to the ultimate source of information in the universe: Google. With a few strokes on the old keyboard, I quickly learned that "clean business is good business." So is good health, being human, good user experience, sustainability, and good design. And that was just on page 1 of my search. Page 2 added smart giving, doing good, and responsibility.

Curious, I continued.

A second chance for ex-prisoners? Good business. God's business, according to a 1974 episode of the television sitcom *Good Times*, is also good business. The same goes for hiring veterans, education, empowering women, paid family leave, food safety, and diversity.

Turns out, lots of things are "good business."

Not listed on the first several pages, however, were some pretty basic concepts in business. Good record keeping didn't pop up until page 5. Good service showed up on page 9. And what about making a profit? Seems pretty important to a good business, right? Ten search pages in and never a reference to that one. I guess that's pretty obvious, so no one feels compelled to write about it.

If you want to sell your business to some other business, then branding what you sell as a "good business" appears to be a popular strategy. Maybe that's because there's lots of interest in what it takes to run a good business. After all, bad businesses don't tend to stay in business, and no one is in business to go out of business.

So when I tell you that love is just damn good business, am I just adding to a long list of things that are good business? By no means! Love is far greater and far more powerful than just another thing that is one part of a good business—it is *the thing* that makes all the other things either possible or more powerful. It's the starting point from which good business begins and the fuel that drives it toward a meaningful destination. It doesn't matter if you measure a business strictly by its profits, by its social impact, or by some combination of the two: *Love is just damn good business.*

THE MEASURE OF LOVE

I'm going to go out on a short limb here and suggest that many business leaders, perhaps even most of them, don't really understand how love fits into business and why it really matters.

Leaders often don't prioritize love as a business concept because love isn't something they can measure. If they can't measure it, they were taught in classic Peter Drucker style, it can't be managed or improved.

Measuring the results of love on your business, however, isn't as difficult as you might think. In fact, Mara Klemich, who has a

PhD in clinical neuropsychology, has led a team that has spent nearly 20 years researching what drives effective behaviors. She and her husband, Stephen Klemich, have used that research to create and validate a love-centric Heartstyles assessment that measures the effectiveness of 16 key "thinking styles."

Their findings have shown that pride or fear, both of which are self-promoting and self-protecting, are at the heart of eight ineffective thinking styles. They are at the root of behaviors characterized as sarcastic, controlling, easily offended, or dependent.

Do you want those in your leadership? Or in your organization?

Of course not. Instead, you want the eight effective thinking styles, which, surprise, surprise, result from humility and love. These styles are authentic and reliable, and they create personal growth, encourage others, demonstrate compassion, and lead to growth in others.

The Klemiches' "life indicator" assessment describes where you are along a scale of effectiveness. Measuring behaviors and the thinking styles that drive them will help you manage and improve them. In other words, if you are aware that your behaviors are driven by prideful or fearful thinking, you can take corrective action and work on behaviors that are driven by humility and love. Those behaviors are not only nice to have. They are also more effective.

REACTIONS TO LOVE

When I talk about the value of love to a business (which I do roughly 365 days a year), there are usually three basic reactions.

One is from leaders who believe love has no place in business. None. They don't want to say that too loudly because it sounds harsh and cold, and they are PR savvy enough not to make that mistake. But when it comes right down to it, they believe business is brutal and that decisions should be driven primarily by logic. Love, they reason, is an emotion, and, according to Tina Turner, a second-hand one, at that. The idea of incorporating love into the mix does nothing but clog the gears of progress with sentimental hoo-ha that stunts growth, decreases revenues, and slows profits.

Even if these leaders agree in spirit, they reject the idea in practice. They think it is idealistic, naïve, and impractical. So they don't spend much time cultivating love at work. Where do they focus? Technology. A study by Korn Ferry found that 63 percent of the 800 leaders they interviewed said technology will be their firm's greatest source of competitive advantage within five years. And 67 percent said technology will create greater value in the future than people create.[1] These are leaders of multi-million-dollar global organizations, by the way. Are they wrong? Well, not entirely. Technology is important. But they still need to cultivate love.

The second reaction I typically get when I talk about love as good business is from leaders who see love as something needed in business because, well, love is a good thing. It makes the world go 'round. These leaders don't really believe love is intrinsically good business, but they believe love is intrinsically important, and, therefore, the business must sacrifice at times to honor the high principle of love.

Frankly, I think most people fit in that category.

The third group, which I believe is very small but growing daily, understands the bigger reality that love is both intrinsically a good thing *and* actually good for business. They understand that there's never a wrong time to do the right thing and that love is always the right thing. But they also know love isn't some necessary expense that other areas of the business have to carry. It's not a loss leader. It's an investment that produces returns, short term and long term. And they also know that there are times when acting out of love leads to decisions that don't align perfectly with traditional business sense or that cause a dent in short-term results. But they'll tell you that love, like most other business strategies that hold the potential for a reward, involves risks. Unlike other risk-related strategies, however, love never fails. It always produces positive results, and, over time, it makes every other business best practice exponentially better.

I don't encounter the first group as frequently as I once did. In fact, the message of love in business is actually often well received by leaders you might stereotypically think of as data-driven analysts who remind you more of Mr. Spock than Mr. Rogers.

A few years ago, for instance, I gave a presentation to a conference of engineers. I've done a lot of work with engineers and scientists, so I'm well aware of the stereotype, which I can summarize as: "I'm an engineer. I don't do that people thing. Keep the people out of my way, so I can get my job done around here." I know it's not true for most, but it still made me nervous when I was standing in front of about a thousand people from the Internet and telecom industries, talking about love in business. I didn't know if my message was going to fly, so I was being hypersensitive to the body language. From all I could tell from the stage, however, I was connecting with the group, and my message was getting through pretty well. Then, a couple of days later, I got back to my office, and I had an e-mail from somebody in that group who was a manager of LAN technicians. You know, network guys.

"Hey, Farber," he wrote. "You know that love stuff you were talking about? You're right on, man. I've been telling my guys this since the day I became a manager 10 years ago. I've told my technicians to make the customer absolutely love you. Take-you-home-to-dinner love you. Meet-the-wife-and-kids love you. Because if the customers love you, you can blow up their building and they'll say, 'Accidents happen.'"

I have to admit, there was a time when I told that story mainly because I thought it was funny. The more I've thought about it, however, the more I see it as truly profound.

I've also come to see this message as universal—it plays well on all continents. I wasn't always sure of this, especially the first time I gave a major presentation in the Middle East. I wasn't sure if crickets lived in those deserts, but I fully expected to hear them when I started talking about love as a business principle during the Leaders in Dubai Conference in the United Arab Emirates.

This was one of those big-time conferences that every keynote speaker wants to work. The other presenters included Archbishop Desmond Tutu, Benjamin Zander, Gary Hamel, Chester Elton, Jack Perkowski, David Plouffe, and Al Gore. Like them, I knew I had a valuable message to share. That's why I'm in this business. But I wasn't sure how well this particular audience would receive my ideas.

Frankly, this became a great example of a time when I needed to practice what I preached. My LEAP model of Extreme Leadership stands for love, energy, audacity, and proof, and it felt a bit audacious to speak to these hard-core business leaders about why love should be a core component of their strategy. Given their cultural business norms, would they buy what I'm passionate about selling? But we ended up having a lively debate about the role of love in the workplace. There was a point when I felt sure I had lost them, but that was never really the case. The response was respectful and engaged, the discussion was stimulating, and the people were warm, friendly, and gracious. No crickets.

I had a similar experience in Singapore, which boasts the second-most competitive economy in the world, according to the World Economic Forum. Singapore has a culture highly driven by self-preservation. When asked how they saw Singapore's society, the top response by Singaporeans in 2015 was *kiasu*, which means "afraid to lose," followed by competitive, materialistic, self-centered, and *kiasi* ("afraid to die"). The responses painted a picture of a self-focused culture that would actively resist love as a business principle. But in the same survey, Singaporeans also said their top personal values were family, responsibility, friendship, happiness, health, and caring.[2] They apparently aren't as fatalistic and selfish as they think they are.

I spoke to the Singapore Institute of Management primarily about my love-based mentoring model called Greater Than Yourself. I found it not only aligned with their personal values but it also provided an avenue for reshaping the way so many of their peers see their society. It allowed them to remain competitive as individuals and as an economy, while expressing their desire to help the people around them. Instead of leading as if they were afraid to lose, it showed them how to love others and still play to win.

Recently, I delivered the opening keynote at the global conference for BNI (Business Network International). Gathered in Bangkok, the audience was composed of 3,000 people from 75 countries, and my talk was simultaneously translated into eight languages. It was a great multicultural experiment: would such a diverse group of leaders connect with the idea of operationalizing love as a competitive business practice?

Answer: hell, yes. I stuck around for the whole conference, and for the next three days I had enthusiastic conversations with people from India, Thailand, China, Singapore, Australia, the United Kingdom, Japan, Finland, Denmark, the United Arab Emirates, the United States, and many more—all of whom told me with great excitement that they felt inspired and emboldened to put into practice something that they had intuitively and instinctually known but hadn't acted on: love as a business strategy.

Now, I'm not going to claim that every individual human being at that conference agreed with and embraced the love-in-business challenge, but I can tell you this with no exaggeration: every culture did.

So my experience tells me that leaders around the world are receptive to the idea of love as damn good business, but most of them still fit into the category that thinks of it as an overhead expense rather than a revenue driver.

I don't know which of the three groups I mentioned fits best with your thinking, but I know where I want you to be by the time you finish this book. Heck, I really want you to be there by the time you finish this chapter. Like, right now. Then the rest of the book will provide the power by showing you how this idea can work for you as a leader and in your organization.

In fact, my team and I have created a little tool to help you get started. It's a preassessment that's 100 percent free (except, you know, for whatever you shelled out for this book). Go to www.loveisgoodbiz.com. Here's your code: loveisgoodbiz. Use the results to create a baseline for where you are, and then read the rest of the book not only to understand the topic but also, and more important, to understand where you want to go as a leader and how you can get there.

2

THE COMPETITIVE
ADVANTAGE

*I look into their eyes and I try to figure out whether they love the
money or they love the business. Everybody likes money. If they
don't love the business, I can't put that into them. . . . We count on
people loving the business. Then my job is to make sure that I don't
do anything that in effect kills that love of the business.*
—WARREN BUFFETT

A BUSINESS FRAMEWORK FOR LOVE

I f you're an aspiring leader in this crazy world, you probably
wake up many nights thinking about the daunting task that's
staring you down. You've noticed that the world's a bit messed up.
It's complicated. And complex. Lots of moving parts that somehow must fit together if everything is going to work out well. And
it's a world with lots of storms—and I don't mean only the climate-
related ones. I mean political storms. Cultural storms. Technology storms. Cross-generational storms. Storms of change. Dark,
ominous storms. Cold, emotionless storms.

To survive these storms as a leader, you have to be "emotionally intelligent" and "full of grit." You have to be an expert in your

field, beaming with self-confidence, while humble and collaborative. You have to provide vision and direction, while empowering
everyone to do their own thing. You have to be firm and flexible.

And you have to, you know, win.

You can define winning however you want, but your success
as a leader hinges on your ability to achieve the definition you've
created and/or agreed to live with. It might be a written definition, it might be implied, or it might be a little of both. But written or not, it exists.

In today's business environment, most leaders are held accountable for some level of personal and organizational social responsibility. That's become part of what it means to win. That's
considered *good business*. But there's also a financial component
to most definitions. You win by making a profit, for instance, or by
hitting goals for growth. That's capitalism.

There's been a rise in the idea, especially among millennials
and generation Z folks, that it's time to scrap capitalism in favor
of something they see as more people friendly, like socialism. It
sounds good, and it motivates the crowds on some college cam-
puses, but that's not the answer. Socialism, history tells us, hasn't
worked out well for the people it purports to save. Not that capitalism has a perfect track record. But as Mark Perry, a professor of
economics and finance at the University of Michigan, succinctly
put it, "The main difference between capitalism and socialism is
this: Capitalism works."[1]

It might not be perfect, but it's better than anything else
that's been tried, and it can be better than its current self if those
who practice it will simply add one ever-important ingredient:
love.

Socialism fails because it doesn't address the human need
for individual incentives, but capitalism becomes exponentially

greater when its incentives are grounded in and guided by love (as opposed to avarice, selfishness, and all the other motivators that give capitalism a black eye).

Love, of course, comes with its own cargo bay full of baggage, so it's really important that we go no further without discussing what I mean by love and how it fits in the context of leadership and business.

There's a book by Bill Bryson—*The Mother Tongue*—that word-nerds love because it's all about this amazing tool we use called *language*. In a section about jargon, Bryson points out that a conference of sociologists back in 1977 provided this inspiring, fluffy, sugary definition of love: "the cognitive-affective state characterized by intrusive and obsessive fantasizing concerning reciprocity of amorant feelings by the object of the amorance."

I share that not only because it's hilarious but also because it's a great example of what I'm *not* talking about. Whatever that definition means, I'm confident it is far different from what I (and you) mean when we use the word.

C. S. Lewis, in *The Four Loves*, helped sort through the confusion around the various meanings of love. He pointed out that the ancient Greeks used four different forms of the word, and all four have made their way into our modern language and thinking: *eros* ("romantic"), *storge* ("affection"), *philia* ("friendship"), and *agape* ("charity").

Eros is the hunger you and your significant other feel toward each other (hopefully).

Storge is how you describe your feeling for that old T-shirt you wore in college the day your team beat that other team that you really, really hated.

Eros at work will likely land you in a world of legal troubles. *Storge* is nice, but it lacks meaningful punch in the business world. *Philos* and *agape*, however, are powerful. They describe love as something more than a sentiment, and go into the territory of a discipline—something you can practice.

Philos is a deep version of friendship—the brotherhood or sisterhood knitted together by a common cause and values. This isn't a casual friendship. Theologian John Piper once described it as a relationship in which "two people are linked arm in arm, shoulder to shoulder, with a common vision and a common goal and a delight and a partnership pulling together toward the goal."[2] This is very different, obviously, from *eros*. Lewis put it this way: "Eros will have naked bodies; friendship naked personalities."[3] In other words, there's a vulnerability and transparency that's inherent in the deep friendship referred to as *philos*.

Agape, meanwhile, is divine love, the deepest, most unconditional expression of the word. It represents selfless sacrifice for the good of someone else, even if, perhaps especially if, the other person doesn't deserve it or can't repay it. While we can't expect to express the God-version of *agape* since, well, you know, none of us is God, we can express an imperfect human version of it. And even though the word refers to the "divine," this kind of unconditional love—a love that expects no quid pro quo—does not require a belief in God to be practiced. This version exists (hopefully) between spouses, as well as between parents and their children and between others with significantly deep bonds. But it also can exist between strangers. It's the love that compels us to volunteer at a homeless shelter or rush to the aid of victims of a natural disaster.

Imagine *philos* and *agape* as the heartbeat of your leadership—as the love that flows from and throughout you, your teams, and your organization. Those forms of love will actually produce radically great business results.

But I hear (or at least can anticipate) the questions that are ringing in your head: "How so? How do philos and agape lead to market share or profits or any of my other hard-core business goals? How do we win in business with love?"

Good questions.

Here's the simple answer: it's because love provides a timeless competitive advantage.

Leaders throughout the business world are always searching for the ever-elusive competitive advantage that will help their organizations succeed, not just for one or two transactions but over the long haul. Years. Decades. Generations, even.

Love provides that advantage.

When love is part of an organization's framework, employees and customers feel genuinely valued. Employees are more loyal, innovative, creative, and inspired. They are then more likely, in a meaningful and sustainable way over time, to produce products, services, and experiences that their customers will love. As a result, customers reciprocate with their loyalty, referrals, and, of course, money. Healthy employee relationships and customer retention, combined with the growth and abundance associated with love-based decisions, make for an overall healthy and successful business.

Love is the first and foundational component of the LEAP model of Extreme Leadership (Love, Energy, Audacity, and Proof) that I developed and that I've taught to leaders and throughout organizations for more than 20 years. To better explain the competitive advantage love creates, I need to tell you a little about this model.

I believe real leaders approach the act of leadership the way you would approach an extreme sport like ice climbing, snowboarding on a half-pipe, or cliff diving. These are scary things that some people choose to do. They aren't forced to do them. There's just something about these sports they love. They embrace the fearful moments that come with meaningful leadership—what I like to call OS!Ms, or "Oh, shit! moments."

Leadership is also scary, when done well, and it's always something you must choose. If you're going to take on the challenge of Extreme Leadership, you're going to need love because love is the ultimate motivator: love generates energy, inspires audacity, and requires proof.*

Putting love into action in ways that create a competitive advantage isn't always easy, but it's not complicated. In fact, it's simple. Here's the formula: do what you love in the service of people who love what you do.

Let that soak in a little:

> Do what you love
> in the service of people
> who love what you do.

I regularly speak to business audiences around the world, and nothing resonates more with them than that simple, yet profound line. It's the most quoted thing I've ever said or written. People respond to it, partly because it's catchy but mainly, I believe, because they intuitively know it's true. They love learning why it's true, why it matters, and how they can make it live within their leadership style and throughout their organizations.

To explain how it works, I start with the end goal: creating a competitive advantage by providing products and services that people love.

---

* Shameless promotional plug: I'll discuss Extreme Leadership and the LEAP model throughout this book, but you also can buy *The Radical Leap* online and at fine bookstores everywhere.

Over the last 20 or so years, one of the ways businesses have sought a competitive advantage is by providing great customer experiences. Once upon a time, this was a radical idea. Way back in 1982, one of my mentors, Tom Peters, published the groundbreaking book *In Search of Excellence*. Tom and his coauthor, Bob Waterman, made the case that company leaders should get "close to the customer" and actually take the customer's experience into consideration when figuring out their strategy. The company, in other words, should build itself around the customer experience.

In the early 1980s, mind you, their idea of a creating a "satisfied customer" was cutting-edge thinking. Now, however, customer satisfaction doesn't mean squat. It's important; don't get me wrong. But there's virtually no correlation between a satisfied customer and repeat business or a customer recommendation. Why? Because satisfactory customer service has become a baseline expectation. It's table stakes. With it, you are merely in the game. It takes more to actually win. A lot more.

Think about it in terms of, say, a restaurant. If you go to an upscale seafood restaurant, you have certain expectations. You expect a really good meal, of course, but you also expect a nice ambiance, a friendly waitstaff, maybe some good music. If you get those experiences, you walk out satisfied. And the next time you want to go to an upscale seafood restaurant, or you want to recommend one to a friend, this one will be on your list. But so will several others—the ones you've tried and enjoyed and probably a few you've heard about but haven't yet visited.

So what would make you pick one over the other? You'll pick the one you love the most, and the *love* factor will involve those aspects that went above what you expected and that touched you in a special way. It's probably not one thing but a combination.

Maybe you know that the chef teaches cooking classes to students at an urban public high school. Maybe the busboy who took away your crumb-covered bread plate had such a look of joy on his face that you felt compelled to ask him a question about why he likes working there. His answer inspired you because it's all about the gratitude he has for his employer and the way he's treated with respect and dignity. Maybe the waitress addressed you by name every time after the first introduction, and while she didn't pry or hover, she was engaging in ways that went beyond learning your choice of salad dressing.

When customers love your business—your products, your services, your people, and the other things that make your business stand out—that's when something great happens. That's when you see repeat business. That's when you get customer loyalty. That's when you create raving fans. That's when you experience the power of forgiveness. That's when you get an advantage over your competition. And that's why leaders should aspire to create an experience that customers love.

Creating that type of experience, however, isn't something an organization can fake. Slapping a snazzy tagline on a website and blasting out some well-written tweets might make a good initial impression, but those won't survive the test of time. A deeply valued customer experience has to come from employees who love what they're doing.

You hear and read a lot these days about the importance of employee engagement, but here's the reality. Over the 10-year period from 2008 to 2018, employee engagement scores among US companies rose a grand total of 3 percent.[4] During that time, companies spent more than $1 trillion on leadership development.[5] My point? Whatever they're teaching for all that money, it's lacking in love. Because employees will love what they're doing only if their leaders love what they are doing and create a culture where love can thrive.

That's why leaders have to do what they love in the service of people who love what they do. This nips narcissism in the bud by moving the focus to a shared vision and to the people who help carry it out. It provides the moral and ethical context to go with the business construct. It's not serving others out of obligation or self-interest but out of a genuine desire to have a huge positive impact on the quality of their lives. And if you do that, what comes back? They reciprocate. They love you in return. That's how you create an engaged culture that bakes love into the customer experience, creates a lasting bond, and produces a competitive advantage.

BANKING ON LOVE

I was in Boston a few years ago to speak to the senior management team of what was then known as Sovereign Bank. This was a new client, so my preparation and research included some time on the phone talking to senior executives to learn about the company—its values, its competitive landscape, its objectives, its key strategies, and its biggest challenges. It was educational, and I felt prepared, but I had never been inside a Sovereign Bank. It was a regional bank based in Boston, and I lived in California.

I arrived a day early, however, and an opportunity presented itself to do a little field research. I had some documents I needed notarized, so I asked the hotel concierge where I could get that done. He pointed to the bank across the street from the hotel, a branch of Sovereign Bank. Naturally, I walked over.

There were two tellers on duty, so I asked one of them if the bank had a notary.

"That would be Rosella," she said, pointing me to the other teller. "She will take care of you."

I stepped over to Rosella's window, and we started doing the usual notary thing, signing this, stamping that. She was a lovely person, and we engaged in typical small talk. I didn't say anything to Rosella about why I was in town. I didn't tell her anything about my philosophy of leadership. It was sign this, stamp that, and small talk. That was it. When she finished her work, I asked her a question that I've asked every notary I've ever used: "What do I owe you?"

"Oh, no," she said. "You don't owe me anything. This is just a service that we provide to our customers."

"Well, that's very nice, Rosella," I told her, "but I'm not a customer of this bank."

"Oh, that's OK," she said. "Maybe you will be someday."

I thought, "Hey, you know. That's pretty good." Then I was struck with this inspiration to ask a question that in retrospect seems pretty obvious: "Rosella, can you do me a favor?" I said. "Would you mind telling me, how do you like working at Sovereign Bank?"

There was no hesitation. Her face lit up, and she said, "I love it!" Then she started telling me, with great enthusiasm, I might add, about the other banks where she had worked and how different they were from the supportive culture that she worked in now. She started talking about how great her customers were and how sometimes they stopped in just to say hello, even when they didn't have any banking business to conduct. She was going on and on, and I was taking notes on the back of one of the documents that I had just signed.

Here's one of the things she said to me, and it's an actual quote that I jotted down on one of those documents: "I love my customers, and I get great pleasure from serving them, so I'm happy."

She was describing the cyclical effect of love. *When I love them, it's easy for me to take care of them, which makes me happy. The happier I am, the better I can take care of them, which, of course, they love.* And on and on it goes.

At one point it became obvious that I would want to share much of what she was saying, so I asked if I could quote her.

"Would you like me to notarize it?" she said.

She took out a business card, flipped it over, wrote "I love my customers," stamped it, signed it, and pushed it across the counter to me. I ran back to my hotel across the street and took a picture of it with my iPhone, then stuck the photo in the presentation I was giving the next day to all of those people Rosella worked for.

"Hey, check this out," I told the executives. "Look what you have going on right across the street. This is Rosella, the tellah." (I was in Boston, remember). "She's awesome."

Then I recapped my notary adventure. The boss was so blown away by this story that he went across the street to say thank you to Rosella. Can you imagine how she reacted? How that affected her day? How that added to the cyclical effect generated by love?

So please don't tell me love has no place in business. Of course, it does. We can dance around it and call it other things like "passion" or "enthusiasm," but the bottom line is that it's a connection of the heart, human being to human being. It's love.

INVESTING IN LOVE

But you still might be wondering if love really adds value to a business. Warren Buffett sure thinks it does. You've probably heard of him. He's done pretty well financially by making a few wise investments in companies. Indeed, he's generally regarded the best ever at making savvy investments.

One day I came across a video interview with him on the *Motley Fool* website. They asked him a question I'm sure he's heard a million times about how he determines whether a company is worth buying. And he gave the answer you'd expect. He talked about analyzing the numbers (for which he has a legendary, uncanny ability) and reviewing the competitive landscape and doing his due diligence on the management team. But if all of that comes up good, he still has one more step. He sits down with the CEO and looks for the love.

"I look into their eyes, and I try to figure out whether they love the money or they love the business," Buffett said. "Everybody likes money. If they don't love the business, I can't put that into them." If they do love it, he said, then "my job is to make sure that I don't do anything that in effect kills that love of the business."[6]

It's not hard science, I know, but if you analyze Buffett's 15-second answer, he uses the word *love* four times. Buffett knows love matters, because he knows that we, as human beings, do all we can to nurture and grow the things we love. If he sees dollar signs in the CEO's eyes instead of love, then Buffett knows that the only thing this person is interested in is his exit strategy. He or she is likely thinking, "How quickly can I stuff this money into my pockets and get the hell out of here?" But Buffett is looking to invest in an asset that's going to grow over time, and there's no way that's going to happen unless the love is there.

That, by the way, includes leaning into the side of love many of us don't like to discuss: tough love. If you have children or if you were a child at one time—so, you know, all of us—then you've experienced tough love. Or maybe you've experienced it from a friend. Or a coworker. Or a boss. Tough love is that component of love that compels us to do the hard, right thing. It can create tension, maybe even some conflict. But the *love* part allows you to work through it effectively because the goal isn't to satisfy your pride or feed your need for control or placate any other selfish motive. It's to do what's in the best interest of the other person and the team as a whole.

Real love doesn't produce organizations where everyone is happy all the time, where people walk around with big, goofy grins on their faces, where no one ever argues, where everybody does whatever they want whenever they please, where every so often you stop all the action and have a group hug in the breakroom or gather around a campfire to roast marshmallows and sing *kumbaya*. Not that I'm against any of those things, especially if the marshmallows come with graham crackers and chocolate. But real love includes accountability and sets an expectation of excellence.

Here is a simple formula: kindness + high standards = love at work.

Company cultures rooted in love demonstrate mutual care and concern for one another's needs, hopes, dreams, and aspirations. People treat each other with the dignity and respect that is called for on virtually every values statement in every company on every part of the globe. When people treat each other with kindness, they are more helpful and thus more productive. And kindness generates these same feelings for customers and clients; it cultivates an organization that cares for the people it serves.

Kindness, however, is just one part of the equation. Sometimes love for the health of the company and love for the individual employees smack right up against each other. Sometimes love is tough. That's because real love is driven by a commitment to excellence. High standards create a vision people can believe in and support, one they can love. That love generates a commitment to excellence in the products and services they create, in the ways they create them, and in the manner in which they treat each other. And they set standards for accountability driven by love and executed with kindness.

Think about it: When you love people, you want what's best for them. You don't settle for mediocre. You strive for excellence. That means there are times when you will have to make tough decisions and have some difficult conversations.

Chris Myers, CEO and cofounder of BodeTree, came face-to-face with this while managing a workforce that was made up largely of millennials like him. Organizational kindness that allowed for flexible work hours led to a pattern of short workdays—people arrived late but then, as he put it, "looked like Fred Flintstone sliding down the back of the dinosaur" when 5 p.m. rolled around. So he gathered everyone for a conversation about their shared commitment to high standards.

"When we do the right thing on our own, the freedoms we enjoy as a team expand," he said. "When we abuse what freedoms we have, they get reduced."[7]

The conversation wasn't fun, but it worked because it was delivered with kindness. With love.

When leaders like Myers do what they love in the service of people who love what they do, they create a competitive advantage, and everyone wins. And that's what the rest of this book will help you learn to do. It's broken into three parts, each covering a section of that mantra: Part I, "Do What You Love," Part II, "In the Service of People," and Part III, "Who Love What You Do." Each part includes a chapter on "the big idea," a chapter of case study illustrations, and a third chapter that's loaded with practical takeaways that will equip you to lead with the kind of love that makes for damn good business.

DO WHAT
YOU LOVE

Yes, love as a business principle will yield remarkable business results, but at its core, it's a deeply personal thing. Leaders need a love for their work—a passion for the business they're running, the people they're running it with, the future they are envisioning, and the values their organization stands for.

Passion is lived in different ways by different personalities and in different corporate and national cultures, but it's always a personal approach to leadership. This section will help you understand the importance of loving what you do, how to identify what you love, and how to demonstrate that love.

3

I NEVER HAVE TO WORK,
YOU SAY?

*You have a masterpiece inside you, too, you know. One unlike any
that has ever been created, or ever will be. And remember:
If you go to your grave without painting your masterpiece, it will
not get painted. No one else can paint it. Only you.*
—Gordon MacKenzie

THE BIG IDEA: DO WHAT YOU LOVE

You've probably spent countless sleepless nights wondering why Samuel Pierpont Langley failed in his effort to build the first working airplane or why Clarence Chamberlin or Richard Byrd didn't win the Orteig Prize by making the first nonstop transatlantic flight from New York to Paris.

No? Not even one sleepless night wrestling with those questions?

That's OK. But these two aviation history stories have something in common that's worth a few minutes of our attention, and it won't cost you any sleep.

Langley was a well-known astronomer, physicist, and aviation pioneer with an outspoken personality. He raised a considerable amount of money, including $50,000 from the US War Department and $20,000 from the Smithsonian, to fund his efforts to build the first piloted "flying machine." But, as you probably know, that honor went to Orville and Wilbur Wright. The Wright brothers, little-known bicycle makers from Ohio, made history on December 17, 1903, with a flight that lasted all of 59 seconds over the sand dunes of the Outer Banks in North Carolina, which thus earned the right to one day put "first in flight" on its license plates.

A couple of decades later, Byrd earned fame with his well-funded flight over (or at least somewhere near) the North Pole in 1926. Chamberlin, meanwhile, was known for his daredevil aviation stunts, and he had set a new flight endurance record (more than 51 hours in the air) in 1927. Both were well known and well financed, so they were heavy favorites to win the $25,000 Orteig Prize. Instead, a little-known airmail pilot named Charles Lindbergh beat them both to Paris.

What links these stories together in my mind is one word: *motivation*. Langley, Chamberlin, and Byrd all achieved great things during their lives. But when it came to these particular pursuits, many historians believe they were largely motivated by fame. Ego and pride were side-tracking factors that limited their success. The Wright brothers and Lindbergh, meanwhile, surely had an interest in fame, but one of their primary motivators was their intense passion for advancing aviation.

The fact that they were doing what they loved didn't guarantee their success, but it fueled their efforts. And in these two examples, it helped them beat the heavily favored competition.

This commitment to doing what you love as a leader is the foundational first step in an Extreme Leader's journey.

THE HARD WORK OF WORK

The great philosopher Anonymous once pointed out that if you choose a job you love, you'll never have to work a day in your life.

Yeah, I know what happens if you Google that quote. Many websites attribute it to Confucius, the great Chinese philosopher and teacher who lived from 551 BC to 479 BC. Shocking as it might sound, there are times when you can't trust everything you read on the Internet. Dig a little, and you'll discover that there's no source to back the claim that this pearl of wisdom came from Kong Qiu (as Confucius is known in China).

Some attribute it to Mark Twain. Seems reasonable, like something he might have said. But still not provable.

Who then?

Author and businessman Harvey Mackay deserves credit for popularizing the saying, but there's evidence that unidentified "others" said it before he did. So Anonymous emerges as the safest bet.

There's a much bigger question, however, than the source of this quote: is it actually true?

The sentiment seems to be that doing what you love for a living somehow magically transforms everything about it into tasks that are always easy, fruitful, and fun. Nice as that seems, it's a bit like attributing the quote to Confucius. It's just not true.

I know a guy who spent years working in the rodeo as a bullfighter. He loved what he did, but not so much the times when he was stepped on, kicked, or gored by an 1,800-pound bull. I love what I do. I know hundreds of people who love what they do. I don't know anyone, including me, who never experiences difficulties from work—even if they aren't as life threatening as an angry bull. On the surface, my job is nothing like the bullfighter's. Yes,

I'm kind of stepping into the bull ring when I'm delivering a keynote, but I'm never going to get gored or stomped on (not literally, anyway). The most dangerous part of my job is the risk of being onstage and my pants falling down in front of a thousand people.

I read a blog post once in which the author called the quote in question an "absurd axiom" and a "blatant, hurtful lie that far too many people fall for."[1] I wouldn't go that far, but I will suggest that well-meaning catchy sayings, when closely examined, often unintentionally open cans of worms that end up eaten by the early birds.

But here's the thing: I don't believe Mackay or Twain or Confucius or anyone else who ever uttered or might have uttered some version of that quote actually meant or believed that doing what you love eliminates the hard work of work. They weren't saying that doing what you love transforms work into play. This was Twain's point in *The Adventures of Tom Sawyer* when he wrote that "Work consists of whatever a body is obliged to do. Play consists of whatever a body is not obliged to do."

And besides, sometimes *play* is hard work too. Ask Tom Brady or Steph Curry or Bryce Harper . . . or anyone else who has made a career out of playing a game. Or ask yourself. If you have a hobby that you or others look at as "play," chances are you have to work hard to do it well.

Arnold Palmer, who played golf so well they named a drink after him, had this to say about the sport he mastered: "Golf is deceptively simple and endlessly complicated; it satisfies the soul and frustrates the intellect. It is at the same time rewarding and maddening—and it is without a doubt the greatest game mankind has ever invented."

Clearly, he loved golf, but it was hard work, sometimes frustrating, and not always fun.

One component of my work involves writing. Blogs, white papers, this book. Writing, for me, is fun. I love it. But I also can relate to the words of legendary sportswriter Red Smith: "Writing is easy. All you do is sit down at a typewriter* and open a vein."[2] Or to quote another great writer, Nathaniel Hawthorne, "Easy reading is damned hard writing."[3]

The philosophers and/or pseudophilosophers who have said that choosing a job you love means you'll never have to work a day in your life have all known that work is sometimes tedious, frustrating, challenging, difficult, boring, and otherwise little to no fun. They were simply saying that by doing what you love, you will experience more contentment and joy in what you're doing.

I think this is similar to the "happiness-at-work" movement that's gained some momentum over the last decade or so. There are all sorts of books about happiness at work, and you can even take courses like "The Science of Happiness at Work" at prestigious universities like Cal-Berkeley. But André Spicer, a professor at the Cass Business School in London and the author of *Business Bullshit*, and Carl Cederström, an associate professor at Stockholm University, point out that we're quick to ignore research about happiness at work when it doesn't fit our happy narratives. For starters, they say, "Measuring happiness is about as easy as taking the temperature of the soul or determining the exact color of love."[4] Some myth-busting research, they say, also shows happy employees actually aren't more productive, that the pursuit of happiness can be an exhausting burden, and that happiness can lead to selfishness and loneliness.

---

* Note to readers under the age of 30: A typewriter is what writers used before laptops, tablets, and phones, which, by the way, once were devices used exclusively to make telephonic calls.

Despite all of that, I have to say that I'm still prohappiness. If I have to choose between happy and unhappy, I'll always pick happy. But I realize that happiness is circumstantial. We won't always be happy in our work because circumstances don't always support happiness. Joy and contentment are inner qualities we can embrace even if the boss is in a bad mood, we had a flat tire on the way to a big meeting, or the dog chewed up our favorite pair of dress shoes. And when it comes right down to it, I think most happiness-at-work gurus are really talking about contentment or joy. Labeling it "happiness" just makes them happier . . . or more content, if you will.

Many people, on the other hand, have a skewed view of work that goes something like this: Work is something adults must do. If it's not optional, then we can't control it. If we can't control it, then we can't enjoy it. And if we can't enjoy it, then we can't love it. We just have to make the best of it because work is one of those unavoidable realities of life. Whatever fun or enjoyment we find in our work comes *despite* that reality.

In short, work sucks. Deal with it.

There's a technical term for that view of work: *bullshit*.

Many religions of the world, including Judaism and Christianity, teach that work is a calling from God and a form of worship, something that was part of the original plan and that was corrupted when the world fell apart. Whether or not you believe that, you've no doubt experienced the reality that work is inherently difficult and challenging. At the same time, those difficulties and challenges actually help us grow into better, wiser individuals. They teach us. They stretch us. They mold us. Those difficulties and challenges don't prevent us from loving what we do. In fact, they can, if we choose, contribute to our love for what we do.

My guess is that Arnold Palmer would not have loved golf nearly as much if he had never experienced a bad bounce or an unfriendly gust of wind at just the most inopportune time. Overcoming the frustrating and maddening parts of the game is what made him better and, I believe, contributed to his love for playing golf.

Doing what you love, you see, is essential to success in life. Not riches. Success. Those two things can live together, but sometimes they don't live in the same zip code. You don't have to do what you love to make a lot of money. But doing what you love allows you to enjoy your life, make a positive difference in the lives of others, and build a sustainable, profitable business.

SUFFERING FOR LOVE

This book draws a bold conclusion: love is damn good business.

That love must originate in the heart of the Extreme Leader. A leader who doesn't do what he or she loves will never truly make love a core component of the business. So any attempt to include love as an integral part of a business plan begins at a very personal level for the leaders of that business. It begins with this:

Do what you love.

It sounds so romantic, doesn't it? But what does it really mean to "do what you love"?

Many of us are aware of the unfortunate abuse that's befallen the word *love*. We use it to describe so many of our relationships that we've stripped away much of its power and value.

I love hot dogs. I love baseball. I love the beach. I love rock 'n' roll. I love rainy nights. I love what I do.

Extreme Leaders don't do what they love in a flippant, non-chalant way that's driven by their microwaved emotions. Instead, love represents a passion for their work and the people connected to their work. It's the force that inspires them, motivates them, and drives them, regardless of the short-term results, the critics, the challenges, or the ill-timed circumstances of a gust of wind during a golf shot.

This passion is lived out in different ways by different person-alities, but it's always a sacrificial approach to leadership. After all, the word *passion* originates from the Latin words *pati* ("to suffer") and *passio* ("suffering," "being acted upon"). So you know you are doing what you love when you are willing to suffer for it, to sac-rifice for it, to put the best interests of what you do ahead of your temporary comfort or happiness, to find contentment in the jour-ney even when it's taking you down barren roads or back alleys. You know you are doing what you love when the idea of *not doing it* creates an overwhelming sense of emptiness. You can't *not* do it, even if at times it feels like, well, hard work.

Doing what you love, in that sense, is similar to the type of love that leads to a lifelong commitment in marriage. To be clear, you should love the person you marry more deeply and with greater commitment than you love the work you do. But that doesn't mean you can't love both with an incredible passion that creates powerful relationships and life-changing results. In both cases, your love prompts behaviors that are, among other things, self-less, collaborative, sacrificial, patient, kind, humble, calming, grateful, trusting, hopeful, persevering, and protecting.

That type of love never fails. It's challenging and difficult at times, but it also leads to rest, solitude, and reflection. Those are important times in the life of a leader, and we pursue them not just out of love for our self (our physical, mental, emotional, and spiritual health) but out of our love for others and our love for what we do. These reenergizing activities are important parts of work in the life of an Extreme Leader, and, in fact, they are key strategies for helping us discover what it is that we love to do.

In that sense, love is a call to self-discovery. But that self-discovery is followed by a call to actions. *Do what you love* begins with a critical word: *Do*. It's not enough to identify what we love or to talk about what we love or to make plans around what we love. We have to *do* it. We have to put that verb in gear and take actions. And not just ordinary, routine actions. I'm talking about actions that make us uncomfortable. Not just physically uncomfortable, like, say, lifting bales of hay; and not just mentally uncomfortable, like, say, quantum physics or filling out our tax forms. But actions that are emotionally and spiritually hard because love drives out our fears, and taking actions against our fears is its own special kind of hard.

There's a reason *effective leadership* is *Extreme Leadership*. You can't have effective leadership without the risks and fears that take you to the extremes of your comfort zones.

I've said many times that fear and love are two of the most powerful forces in the human experience. The dynamic interplay between those forces is what drives effective leadership. The challenge for Extreme Leaders is to actively and intentionally use them every day in our attempts to change our personal spheres of influence for the better.

That means doing what you love is not only intensely personal but it's also intrinsically scary. It's a calling others may not understand or appreciate. It's a calling to change the nature of things, which means you are asking yourself and others to give up the familiar. It's a calling to pursue goals and dreams without any guarantee of success. It's a calling to risk your pride and reputation in a harsh and judgmental world. It's a calling, in short, that comes with fears.

Fears often paralyze people in leadership positions. They take control and drive a leader to love the things that are self-focused—security, comfort, personal success, money, control, power—significantly more than things that are focused on others. These types of leaders don't do what they love. They love *what they think they can get* out of what they do. Very different.

Our fears fit into three categories: those that warn us of real threats and thus should be respected; those that lie to us and thus should be freed by truth; and those that own us (or attempt to own us) and thus should be conquered by love. The second and third are related because the second often evolves into the third.

The process of freeing ourselves from fear-based lies and conquering the fears that seek to own us can realign us with a greater purpose in life. Doing what you love provides the impetus for engaging that process. You aren't just comfortable with the uncomfortable. You actively seek it. You realize that unless you face your fears and do what is uncomfortable, you can't really lead anyone anywhere worth going. You can't make changes that really matter. And you realize your love for what you do is at the heart of why you're willing to take that risk, why you're willing to face that challenge, why you're willing to push forward even when it makes you uncomfortable.

We have been conditioned to believe that fear is bad, and while it is true that fear can save your life or keep you from doing something stupid, avoiding it can also keep you from doing something great or from learning something new or from growing as a human being. Fear is a natural part of growth, and since growth, change, revolution, reinvention—whatever you want to call it—are all on the leaders' agenda, then fear comes with the leadership territory.

So my contention is simply this: Extreme Leaders live in the daily pursuit of that fear, not for the sake of fear, not for the hell of it, but because they understand that if they are really going to change things, if they are really going to lead people to new ways of doing things, new ways of thinking, new ways of conducting business, new ways of creating relationships with their customers, new ways of working, then those new ways are by their nature scary to pursue.

Why pursue them if they're all so scary? What's the Extreme Leader's ultimate motivation for sticking his or her neck out so frequently?

Love.

That's the simple, basic motivation for working through all that fear. Love makes the fear worthwhile.

To illustrate this interplay between love and fear, think about some activity that you've come to enjoy but that was inherently risky, even dangerous, to learn. The one I typically use is skiing, which is an illustration I originally heard from my mentor, leadership guru Jim Kouzes, coauthor with Barry Posner of *The Leadership Challenge*.

You don't learn to ski by starting on the double black diamond runs. You start on little bunny slopes, fall down a lot in public, and it is a little bit humiliating. But if you are doing it right, you have somebody there who can help you learn why you are falling, and little by little, you develop your skills. In time, you take on slightly bigger slopes that are a little bit scarier, right?

Now, imagine that the day has finally come to really see what you are made of. You are going to take on the double black diamond run, the most difficult slope on the mountain. This is it. The moment of truth has arrived. You look down the abyss, take a breath, maybe say a prayer, and somehow will yourself to push forward—to leap into your fears. Suddenly, you pass the point of no return. There is no turning back. You are 100 percent committed, and that realization brings two words screaming through your mind: *Oh, shit!*

You accept this total gut-wrenching fear when you are learning to ski because you know you can't conquer the mountain by sitting in the lodge with a hot buttered rum in your hand and talking about the latest skiing equipment. You have to strap on the gear and push off the edge. You don't do it because somebody is standing behind you with a shotgun. You accept the risk. You accept the fear. You accept the challenge for one very simple reason: you want to ski. There's something about it that you've come to love.

In my first book, *The Radical Leap: A Personal Lesson in Extreme Leadership*, I gave this example of how this kind of fear plays out at work:

> Now, picture this: you'd been preparing to give a presentation to the executive team of an important prospective client. You and your team had worked for days on the numbers, the graphics, and the perfect words. You had practiced in front of the mirror until it cracked, you had mumbled the entire spiel in your sleep for a week—so says your spouse—and now you're walking across plush gray carpet to the front of the boardroom. You reach the oak podium, turn, and look out at the grim audience of folded arms and Brooks Brothers suits, and you can't run away. Right there in that moment, what are you thinking?[5]

Oh, shit! Right? Those are the words. You have experienced an "Oh, shit! moment," otherwise known as an OS!M. It is the natural built-in human indicator that you are doing or about to do something truly significant, and you are, rightfully so, scared out of your gourd. Don't avoid it. The OS!M, in the right context and for the right reasons, is a good thing. And simply put, your goal as an Extreme Leader is to pursue the OS!Ms.

We have come to believe leadership is just another acquired skill. There are skills involved with leadership, of course—the ability to communicate with people, the ability to give the right kind of feedback, the ability to plan and coordinate, and so on. But we tend to forget about the visceral component. Those skills do not amount to leadership if they aren't used in the pursuit of changing the way things are, and if we use those skills in the pursuit of changing the way things are, we are going to frequently be scared. We are going to experience OS!M after OS!M.

So my argument is simply this: if you are not experiencing that fear, that churning in your gut, then you are not leading yet. And the only way you will consistently push yourself to experience that fear is by doing what you love.

Ultimately, everything the Extreme Leader does is motivated by love for something, someone, or both: love for a principle, love for a cause, love for a product, love for your customers, love for your coworkers, love for a better future, love for the legacy that you leave because of your love for future generations—love, in other words, for people you don't even know.

When you do what you love, it shows up in your vision, your values, your strategies, your tactics—in every plan you make and in every action you take. This leads to big, bold visions and challenging opportunities, but you won't settle for anything less. Because you're doing what you love.

PARACHUTES OF GRATITUDE

Richard Bolles bounced around a bit in his career, and then he turned those bounces into an actual career that allowed him to do what he loved. He spent time in the Navy, and then he studied chemical engineering at MIT before eventually earning a degree in physics from Harvard. And what did he do with those degrees? He became an Episcopal priest, of course. In 1970 he self-published—photocopied, really—a manual to help unemployed ministers find work. That booklet evolved to become *What Color Is Your Parachute?* He updated it frequently, and it became the all-time bestselling book for career guidance. It sold more than 10 million copies, never went out of print, and launched him into a career of helping others find their way on their professional journeys.

A friend of mine once interviewed Bolles at his home office in the San Francisco Bay area. Bolles pointed out that your work might not always be fun, but it shouldn't be devoid of love. He'd seen too many people who thought they were "called" to do something that made them miserable. "There is something wrong with the definition, if one ever comes to it, of saying, 'I'm doing this for God, but I hate it,'" said Bolles, who died in 2017 at the age of 90.[6]

Bolles's universal career advice began with an interesting word: *gratitude*. Not *intelligence*. Not *ambition*. Not *connections*. *Gratitude*. Gratitude for being alive, for being uniquely made, for being able to do work that is unique to you and nobody else. That type of gratitude, he said, leads to joy in your calling.

"When I see people who really feel called to their work," he told my friend, "they get joy out of their work. It doesn't mean there are not stretches when they are tediously plodding through the day. But, basically, they get up alive and excited about what they are doing. They have some sense that there is something unique they have to contribute to this world. This makes them very excited."[7]

In other words, they do what they love.

4

PICTURES OF LOVE

Do ordinary things with extraordinary love.
—MOTHER TERESA

EXPERIENCING THE ENERGY, AUDACITY, AND PROOF

What does it look like to do what you love?

Once I gave a speech to a defense contractor. You know, a company that makes guns, missiles, and other things that go boom. A few days after giving the talk, I got an e-mail from one of the company's sourcing agents. His job was to procure the materials the company needed to make all those products that it sold to its military clients.

He told me that he had recently been tasked with acquiring a material that would help train Marines to deploy a device that would save the lives of many of the country's troops in the field of battle. The supplier said he could have the material in six to eight weeks, but that schedule presented a problem for the sourcing agent. He needed it in one week.

He offered a premium, but the supplier wouldn't budge.

"We couldn't throw enough money at the problem," he told me.

Then he made a critical point to the supplier: "I am not your customer," he told him.

"Our mutual customer was the Marine in the field, whose very life could depend on what we did," he told me in the e-mail. "I do not believe that I was being dramatic, nor was I waving the flag. I simply stated the facts."

That very afternoon, the supplier called back, agreed to provide the material in one week, and ended up beating his own new time frame and delivering in only six days.

"I'd like to think that my skills as a negotiator had something to do with it, but that would be far short of the truth," he told me. "I'm convinced that something much more powerful was at work."

That something, he said, was love. This man has identical twin sons who were veterans of the Marine Corps. Both had been out of the military for 10 years at that point, but a framed 8-by-10 photo of each still proudly stood sentry on his desk.

"When I see them, I can't help but think about all our Marines on duty," he said. "Whenever I see a Marine, it's like seeing my own sons. Maybe it was the genuine love I have for those Marines that came across the phone. After all, you did say love was contagious."

This man's love for his sons and his love for his country inspired a passion within him that made love a critical component in what he did each day and how he did it. That's what it means to do what you love. And, in this case, that love had a direct impact on supply chain efficiency, which made it good for the business.

Did you ever think you would read "love" and a cold, sterile term like "supply chain efficiency" in the same sentence?

Oh, we're just getting started.

BERNIE SWAIN,
WASHINGTON SPEAKERS BUREAU

Doing what you love often is as simple as letting go of everything else. But letting go of everything else is seldom simple or easy. Letting go means you will disappoint people. Letting go means you will be uncomfortable. Letting go means you just might . . . fail.

Bernie and Paula Swain let go.

Bernie was in his early thirties and about to become director of athletics at George Washington University. Not a bad gig, right? Then Harry Rhoads, one of Bernie and Paula's close friends, sent them an article from *Fortune* magazine about the Harry Walker Agency, which at the time was the world's largest speaker agency. The article quoted Henry Kissinger as asking Harry Walker why he should sign with his company rather than a competitor. "We don't have any competitors," Walker told him.

Rhoads had taped a note on that page of the article: "No competitors?" it said.

Paula Swain took that as a challenge and passionately argued that "every life, even ours, needs a great if totally unpredictable and crazy adventure."[1] So with no plan and no experience, the couple quit their jobs and joined Rhoads to give the Harry Walker Agency some competition.

Perhaps you've heard of it: the Washington Speakers Bureau. They have represented almost every person of influence in our modern era—three of the past four US presidents, the last four prime ministers of Great Britain, five secretaries of state, and just about every noteworthy government, sports, military, literary, and business legend. Margaret Thatcher? Check. Ronald Reagan? Check. Colin Powell and Tony Blair? Check, check. Madeleine

Albright, David Brinkley, Lou Holtz, Terry Bradshaw? Check, check, check, and check.

The success of the Washington Speakers Bureau didn't happen overnight, and it didn't happen easily. But it happened, at least in part, because Swain and his partners were doing something they loved. Their passions weren't tossed in the backseat to tag along for the ride. They were the driving force.

Too often, we take a job because the money is good, even though we suspect we'll hate the work. Or we pick a career path to please our parents. Or we get an opportunity that sparks a fire inside of us, but we pass because we're afraid we don't have the skills, talent, or experience to make it successful.

"Passion will drive you to develop the skills, experience, and talent you need to live into your passion," Bernie Swain told me. "Fear is natural, especially in the beginning of a new venture, job, or career. But if the passion is there, you'll be compelled to act in the face of fear."

That's not just advice from some ivory tower. That's based on the Swains' experience. The first headquarters for the Washington Speakers Bureau (WSB) was a closet in someone else's office. And a year after starting their company, they still lacked two pretty important pieces of any business puzzle: clients and revenue. As it turned out, Harry Walker was stretching the truth with his we-have-no-competition statement to Henry Kissinger. There were, in fact, plenty of competitors in the industry, and there wasn't much room for another.

"Many mornings I knew that this would be another day of failure," Bernie Swain said. "But because I believed with my heart and soul in what we were doing, I didn't want to fail. So I drove on."

The agency eventually landed a client (Steve Bell, a journalist at the time with ABC's *Good Morning America*), and then a few more. WSB took on these clients without contracts, meaning (a) the clients could walk at any time and (b) the agency was compelled to work hard and make those clients happy. It did, and its client list began to grow.

After seven years of long days, short nights, and no vacations, WSB experienced a turning point in 1988 when President Ronald Reagan selected the agency to book and manage his speaking engagements after he left office. The Swains later learned that the president had made the decision over the objections of some advisors, picking WSB instead of more established agencies because he liked the fact it was a startup and he wanted to give it a chance.

Reagan no doubt had come away impressed by the grit and determination the Swains and their partners had shown in bootstrapping their company into a true competitor. And I submit to you that it never would have happened if they weren't doing what they loved.

ELISE MITCHELL, MITCHELL COMMUNICATIONS

It's not uncommon for leaders to start off doing what they love but then to veer off course to the point that what they do no longer brings them joy—or, worse, it begins to suck the life out of them. Those leaders don't necessarily need to do something new; they might just need to take up motorcycling.

Well, it worked for my friend Elise Mitchell.

Mitchell is a self-described destination person, and she always has been. Her fierce focus and intense drive helped her build a public relations company from scratch in the northwest corner of Arkansas and sell it 20 years later to Dentsu, Inc., a global marketing communications network with offices in 145 countries. Those same qualities help her to continue to break new ground as CEO of Mitchell Communications and the global Dentsu Aegis Public Relations Network. Chasing the destination helped her achieve phenomenal success, but she realized along the way that her life and her leadership were incomplete. Something was missing in her love for her work.

"I was consumed by reaching the next destination—the next great achievement—and as soon as it was in sight, I already had a list of several new destinations to pursue," Mitchell wrote in her book, *Leading Through the Turn*. "There was no time for rest, no time to soak in the experience of the trip."

Her hard-charging approach eventually took its toll, and she began to battle insomnia as she wrestled with an age-old question: "Is this all there is?"

She avoided the question and the fears that lay beneath it, and, of course, things only got worse. Her life was moving at such a frantic pace that one day she showed up for a client meeting without her shoes. That's when some friends sat her down for an intervention that led to a vacation in Europe. Her husband, a doctor, wasn't keen on going until she offered to make it a motorcycling trip. He loved to ride his motorcycle. She had never ridden, but she agreed to go on the back of his bike through the Alps in Austria, Germany, Italy, and Switzerland. Mitchell fell in love with motorcycle riding on that trip and took it up herself when she returned. It took another two years—and a kitchen table intervention by her husband—but she eventually began making the changes that helped her experience the joy of her journey that paralleled the joy she found in motorcycling.

"First, I admitted that destination leadership had so consumed me that my purpose in life had become defined by my achievements," she wrote. "Then I came to realize that my problem wasn't that I was pursuing unworthy destinations. The problem was that I had missed the journey along the way. In my relentless pursuit of the destination, the journey no longer mattered. I decided that if I could make the journey matter more, then perhaps I could find meaning and purpose for the path I was on—and satisfaction and contentment in my work and in my life."

Mitchell found that riding her motorcycle not only provided a release from the day-to-day stresses of life but it also provided a helpful analogy to guide her path to a more balanced life. Perhaps the most important lesson came from the concept of "looking through the turn." Motorcycle riders have to learn to look where they want to go as they approach a turn, rather than focusing on potential hazards within the turn itself. At the same time, they have to use their instincts and experiences to adjust within the turn. That's the type of balance that allows Extreme Leaders to navigate the challenges of life and work in a healthy manner so that they can enjoy doing what they love.

Mitchell says a journey mindset allows you to reduce the stress and enjoy the ride, but it doesn't mean that the destination doesn't matter. You need both.

"I've learned to be a destination leader with a journey mindset—someone who is still very focused on reaching my goals but who understands that the journey of life is meant to be savored and experienced," Mitchell told me. "This realization has transformed my approach to both my work and personal life, and it's made all the difference."

WERNER BERGER,
MOUNTAIN CLIMBER

I first met Werner Berger when he was 79 years young and on a quest to do something big.

Now, that phrase "years young" might sound like a euphemism, just a nice way of giving his age without calling him, you know, *old*. And there's no doubt that anyone who has made 79 trips around the sun is, in fact, no spring chicken. But Berger's youth remains evident in his attitude and in his lifestyle, and "the quest" I referred to is a prime example: when Berger and I talked, he was preparing to climb Mount Kilimanjaro in Tanzania. With an elevation of 19,341 feet, it's the highest mountain in Africa.

Where else would you want to celebrate your eightieth birthday, right?[2]

Berger already has a spot in the *Guinness Book of World Records* as the oldest person to have climbed the highest mountain on all seven continents, a feat he completed when he was 77. But he wants to do it all again before 2020.

Why?

Climbing mountains is something he loves to do.

Berger didn't discover his love for mountain climbing, however, until he was 55. He was at a workshop when the facilitator asked everyone to identify three things they would love to do before they died but that they'd probably never do. You know, a bucket list. Berger had no experience as a climber. But he was born in Africa, so Kilimanjaro came to mind. Then he thought about the Matterhorn and other beautiful mountains in Switzerland. Then "the lore of Everest kicked in," he said, and he had his goal: visit the base camp of Mount Everest.

He told his family about the goal, and they laughed it off. But two years later, one of his sons brought it up and suggested they take a father-son trip in the Himalayas.

"So we went," he told me. "And for me, it was an incredible experience. In fact, a life-changing experience. Months later, whenever I thought of that trip or I saw a photo of it or I had a conversation about it, this glow came up, and I knew that I wanted to climb higher. I wanted to climb more."

Berger believes the seed for mountain climbing was planted years earlier—on May 29, 1953, in fact. That's when Edmund Hillary and Tenzing Norgay became the first climbers to reach the peak of Mount Everest. Berger was 15 and captivated by the accomplishment. But life rolled on, and the seed spent decades buried somewhere deep within him. The trip to the base camp of Everest—which doesn't require special equipment or training, but does require a certain level of fitness—gave new life to Berger's dream. It was hard, yet exhilarating; challenging, yet fulfilling. Berger quickly realized how much he needed to learn if he was ever to go beyond the base camp, but he also realized, if only at a subconscious level at first, that he had fallen in love with the experience.

"Everything was just so much more beautiful, so much more exciting," he told me. "I ended up feeling so humble in the grandeur of the landscape. And this happened mountain after mountain. To some extent, it was addictive."

When you do what you love, you *have* to do it. And Berger will tell you that applies to your career as well.

Berger had a life before mountain climbing, and it didn't always include a love for what he was doing. After completing master's degrees in science and geology, he ended up taking over a small business and running it so well that he was able to retire at the age of 43. Sweet, right? Many of us wish we could retire (or could have retired) while in our early forties! But for Berger, retirement wasn't nirvana. In fact, he said he "really went into the dumps" for about three years.

"I wasn't retiring to something," he said. "I was retiring from something."

Soak that in a bit because it's really, really insightful.

Berger knew what he *didn't love*—running the business that had provided him with enough financial success to retire at a young age. But he didn't know what he *did love*.

When he brought up his dilemma with a consultant he had met, the consultant suggested he consider . . . consulting. So Berger looked into it and liked what he learned. He could run his own business under the umbrella of a strong organization, and he could help other businesses and their leaders. Berger signed up, got trained and certified, and began his new career. He started out as a consultant on customer service, then began working with middle management, sales teams, and, ultimately, with C-suite executives.

"I ended up being a master trainer in 13 different technologies, which simply means I can train trainers," he said. "And I absolutely loved it."

There's that word again.

One of the many things I admire about Berger is that he enjoys the results regardless of what happens. In business, leaders too often come up with great goals and pursue them with intense passion and focus, but they lack a clear understanding of why they matter. Then they miss the best parts because they find satisfaction only in the accomplishments, not the process.

Berger lived this principle while attempting to climb Denali (formerly known as Mount McKinley), which, at 20,310 feet above sea level, is the highest point in North America. He and his climbing partners were 200 feet from the peak—just another 20 minutes of climbing—when the weather turned nasty. And rather than risk getting caught in a whiteout, Berger's group turned back.

"Everybody was so disappointed for me and wondered how we could possibly quit that close," Berger told me. "And for me, it was just a complete delight. The climb was just spectacular. I cannot even verbalize how phenomenal it was. Getting to the summit would have been nice, but it was absolutely not essential."

He eventually made it to the top of Denali—it took two more tries—but making it or not making it didn't define him or his love for climbing.

"The truth really is that if I had died after my first Denali climb, I would have still been a happy climber," Berger said, "because it was really an awesome experience."

Yet his appreciation for the journey doesn't make him any less competitive. His lack of attachment to the outcome frees him to live with joy in the moment. Combine that with a competitive spirit, and it actually gives him a better chance of achieving his goals. Why? Because he doesn't put himself, his team, or his goals at risk because his ego is consumed by the goal. He's self-aware enough to see the big picture in the middle of the storms.

Extreme Leaders are self-aware, for their own sake and for their teams. And because they do what they love, they won't put the good of the whole at risk just to satisfy or attempt to satisfy an ego-driven goal.

. . . . . .

Leaders like Paula and Bernie Swain, Elise Mitchell, and Werner Berger do what they love, and their lives are all the better for it. But they will tell you that doing what you love doesn't always come easily. Discovering the things you love and then doing them requires, well, hard work. It's a process. A journey. There's no easy flip of a switch that creates this type of self-discovery.

John Ortberg, in *The Life You've Always Wanted*, points out that "there is an immense difference between *training* to do something and *trying* to do something." Trying is good, but training brings intentional, strategic effort to the quest. And that's the next step: investing in the processes that will help you do what you love.

5

HOW TO FALL IN LOVE

Is it so small a thing
To have enjoy'd the sun,
To have lived light in the spring,
To have loved, to have thought, to have done . . .
—MATTHEW ARNOLD

NOW WHAT?

Some university professors had heard so much talk from students about "following your passions" that they decided it was a myth they needed to formally debunk. So they did what all good debunking professors do: they spent their time and someone else's money on research.

Here's how I'd summarize what they discovered: passions aren't found; they're developed.

Those findings run counter to what many believe, the professors said, but to me, it's just common sense. You aren't going to find your passions by kicking over rocks—or by bouncing from job to job until lightning strikes (figuratively speaking, of course). You have to invest some time and energy in the processes of discovery and development. That's how you find what you love to do.

Whether you're just starting out or trying to reignite your passions, you have to take a deep look into your soul, see what's there, and discover how the core of your being relates to the work you will give to the world. This isn't about feeding your narcissistic nature. It's about tapping into your passions so that your life and work truly benefit others—which will bring you more joy and help you build a stronger, more profitable business.

There's no one way to find the answer, but asking introspective questions is a start: "What makes me feel most alive? What do I want to leave as a legacy? What's on my bucket list?" Then give yourself time and space to think through them. Meditate. Go on a retreat. Read. Turn off your smartphone. But you also can find space in your actions. Go for a hike. Play a team sport. Play music with friends. Ride a motorcycle through the countryside. Climb a mountain. Challenge yourself with something *you want to do* but that *you aren't sure you can do*. Get out of your comfort zone, whether it's in solitude or with a group.

The rest of this chapter offers some practical advice, from me and others, on how to take that inward look with a constructive goal of *doing what you love* so that you can serve others who love what you do.

Doing what you love might come to you in a flash, or it might take time to develop as a fruit from years of your experiences, both good and bad. One way you'll know when you've discovered it is that pursuing it will be more important than the actual achievement. The destination will still matter, but it will be part of the journey, not something that replaces the journey.

ADVICE FROM
THE MOUNTAINTOP

This type of self-awareness isn't a one-time event. It's an ongoing part of the trip.

When Werner Berger is on a mountain, for instance, there's a certain level of focus and self-awareness that's essential for his survival. His life literally depends on living in the moment and making decisions that reflect an accurate view of his strengths and his limitations. That same type of focus and self-awareness is essential for Extreme Leaders who want to discover what they truly love to do.

Here are a few questions Berger told me he might ask if he were coaching you in such a quest:

- To what extent do you have a true sense, and maybe a grounded sense, of who you are?

- To what extent do you appreciate your own strengths?

- To what extent do you appreciate and own your limitations?

"Until you are clear on those things, you cannot fully utilize the training that I might have given you in things like communication skills, people skills, or self-management skills," he said. "So your quest becomes to really get to know who you are."

REFLECTING ON PURPOSE

When the destination became the all-consuming, soul-sucking focus of work for Elise Mitchell, she transformed her life in part through rest, solitude, and reflection. Riding a motorcycle was one of the things she did that allowed her to tune out the distractions of her destination-driven world and think about who she was and what she loved.

The transformation didn't come overnight, but it came because she committed time to figuring it out—on her own and with several key people in her life. She didn't change jobs or careers, but she was able to reignite her passions for her work and, in doing so, once again do what she loved.

Mitchell recommends finding your true purpose by looking deeply into the intersections of five areas of your life:

- *Your strengths:* What you are naturally good at doing

- *Your values:* What you believe in

- *Your passions:* The interests that bring you joy

- *Your drive:* What motivates you

- *Your life goals:* What you'd most like to accomplish[1]

"Gaining clarity about purpose can transform your life," Mitchell says. "You can move away from living a taxing and uninspiring life, and move toward a more satisfying and rewarding life."[2]

Take the time to identify and list your strengths, values, passions, drives, and life goals. Write them down. Or try this idea that I got from Elay Cohen, the cofounder and CEO of SalesHood and a former senior vice president of Salesforce.

"About a week after people start here," he told me, "they record a passion video."

What's a passion video? Simple. Turn on the video camera, and record your answer to one question: "What are you most passionate about?"

"People love that stuff here," Cohen said. "They love just getting to know people and really at a human level, really understanding what makes people tick. And folks' passions are spectacular, whether it's someone traveling, playing music, or cooking. . . . Turns out one of our employees has this awesome garden. He goes home every night and goes through his fruit. They're his babies."

Once you know your strengths, values, passions, drives, and life goals, ask yourself how you can more intentionally connect them to your work. You'll be surprised at how often there are connections. But, if nothing else, sharing them with others will help you connect with them and build deeper meaning in your relationships.

LOOKING FOR TURNING POINTS

Bernie Swain, in his book *What Made Me Who I Am*, pointed out that life is a collection of turning points. The path you take is never straight or easy, he wrote, but it can take you—and those you love—somewhere special if you're doing what you love.

To identify and learn from your personal turning points, Swain suggested answering five very personal questions about yourself:

- What have been the defining moments in my life so far?

- What are the principles, values, morals, and experiences that define me?

- Who were or are my biggest influencers, and what did I learn from them?

- What would I pursue even if I were facing almost certain failure?

And to pull all those questions together:

- What makes me who I am?

Answering those questions almost certainly will help you identify what you love so you can do it.

FACING YOUR FEAR

All this self-reflection is likely to lead you to some places that are downright scary. Earlier, I talked about those fear-based lies that keep us from finding and embracing our greater purpose. When we do what we love, we're more willing to face those fears by identifying and embracing what I affectionately refer to as "OS!Ms."

Some OS!Ms are very personal, but many, if not most, are played out in front of the people you interact with at work. As they should be. When you venture out on a limb, even in the face of fear, you send a message that everyone should be pursuing growth. Leaders should relish making mistakes in public. When you show you can publicly acknowledge mistakes made in the effort to grow, people see you as a human being, not a drone, and they will follow you and your lead, and pursue OS!Ms themselves.

You see OS!Ms neatly tucked into the stories of everyone I've mentioned in this section of the book. Mitchell walked away from a busy, growing agency to spend time on a motorcycle with her husband. Later, she sold her company—which had never been the goal when building it—and took a leadership role with the new parent company. Berger not only climbed the highest mountains on the planet—no shortage of OS!Ms there—but he reinvented his professional life with a new career. Bernie and Paula Swain, meanwhile, quit their jobs and, along with their friend Harry Rhoads, started a company that took more than a year and most of their savings before it began to earn them some steady revenue. The way Paula Swain phrased it is worth repeating: "Every life, even ours, needs a great if totally unpredictable and crazy adventure."[3]

We all need these types of OS!Ms. They allow us to identify and face our fears with love-driven actions that bring us joy and inspire the people around us.

How do you recognize an OS!M? When I introduced the idea of the OS!M in *The Radical Leap*, I pointed out that if the only reason you're not taking on a challenge is because the idea scares you, then that's the reason you should take it on. That's your OS!M.

And how do you take on an OS!M? It takes courage. And courage takes love.

Author Brené Brown points out that "*courage* is a heart word" because "the root of the word *courage* is *cor*—the Latin word for heart."[4] When we live courageously, in our words and our actions, it's a reflection of our inner strength that develops by knowing and pursing what we truly love. If you love someone or something from the heart, you're willing to take risks for them or it. Draw on that love, take bold actions, and don't give up when it gets difficult. Because if you want to do what you love, you have to identify and embrace some OS!Ms.

BUT MY WORK SUCKS

"This do-what-you-love stuff sounds great," I hear some of you saying, "but what if I don't love my work?"

There's a reason I say "Do what you love" instead of "Love what you do." Yes, you should bloom where you're planted, and do your best regardless of where you are. But if you aren't doing what you love, you'll always feel like something's missing—because something is missing. Love.

The ideal state for all of us at work—from the C suite to the front line—is to do what we love in the service of people who love what we do. Love brings the fire of creativity to bear on the day to day. It drives loyalty and leaps of innovative brilliance. It pushes us through challenges toward excellence. Developing a strong personal connection to our work is essential to cultivating love in business. Why? Because it's impossible (at least in any significant and long-lasting way) to engage, motivate, compel, energize anyone else unless we first feel it ourselves. But it can't be forced or faked. Cultivated and nurtured, yes. Forced or faked, no.

The thing is, too many of us give up on the idea of doing what we love way too quickly because we've been told for most of our lives that we should do what makes us happy and that if we love what we do, we don't have to work. These and many other nice-sounding adages crumble when they hit the walls of reality.

If you don't like your job, your company, your boss, or the people you work with, don't start by jumping to the conclusion that you're in the wrong place. It very well could be that you are in the wrong place and/or doing the wrong work, but don't start with that conclusion. Instead, use this opportunity to reflect and consider your work in the greater context of your life and goals.

Try the process that follows, and see if it gives you the juice you need to lead in a way that inspires others to accomplish extraordinary things.

1. Remember Why You Took the Job

Reflect on the events, jobs, projects, and other experiences that led you to your current role. Literally draw a map on a piece of paper with "I am here" in the middle of the page. Leave the bottom of the page blank. That represents your future. At the top, draw in some dots to represent the milestone events in your career so far. You might start with your first job or with your high school or college graduation. If you had significant struggles—like getting laid off, failing to meet payroll, or losing a major contract—include those as well. Our setbacks shape us in unique ways, teaching us lessons and motivating us as we move toward new opportunities.

The dots eventually will lead to where you are today, and connecting them will remind you of how and why you got there. Now answer these questions:

- Why did I take this job or start this company or enlist in this program?

- Are the ideals that I started with still in place today?

- If not, how can I re-enliven them?

2. List Every Aspect of Your Current Work, Job, or Career

Make a quick inventory of the various aspects of your work: tasks, projects, roles, responsibilities, colleagues, higher-ups, employees, customers, clients, underlying values. Write them however works best for you.

Draw a circle around the aspects you enjoy, and draw a square around the ones you don't.

3. Highlight Your Gratitude Tree

Use a highlighter to emphasize the items on your list that really resonate with you—those tasks you love doing, the people you truly care about, the values that you strive to live by—and make coming to work worthwhile. Find something—anything—about your work that you do love. (And if "love" is too strong a word for you, I'll accept "like" or "care about." For now.)

Is there a colleague at the office you enjoy working with? Are there particular clients or customers who appreciate the great work you do for them? Is there a role model in your company that you look up to and get inspiration from? Is there something about the principles or mission of your company that you find personally gratifying?

As for the items you don't highlight, well, that's life. Again, we all have tasks we have to do whether we like them (let alone "love" them) or not so that we can continue doing the overall work that we love. I don't love waiting in airports, making sales calls, or tracking expenses, and yet I must do all of those so that I can do what I love about my work. There's a technical term for that. It's called "being an adult."

4. Review Your Highlights Every Day

Once a day—ideally in the morning before the tyranny of the urgent kicks in—review your list and focus on the highlights. Allow yourself to feel genuine gratitude for the things, activities, and people that populate your working experience. That one simple, reflective practice should help to stoke or rekindle the love in your heart for the work you do.

In the day-to-day crush and pressure of work, it's very easy to forget about the good and meaningful elements of our jobs. Yet if we intentionally remind ourselves and focus on them for a time, we'll find that our level of personal satisfaction, energy, and enthusiasm will come back. Sometimes right away.

So next Monday morning, after you brush your teeth and have your coffee, instead of allowing yourself to be overcome with a sense of dread about the imminent workday and week, ask yourself, "What do I love (or at least like) about what I do—about this work [or company, team, project, colleague, or client]?" And if you find that you have absolutely no answer to any variation of that question—not even if you squint—then let me offer a simple, one-word answer to your dilemma:

Leave.

But when you do, make sure you go somewhere you can do what you love—not somewhere that has no problems and where all the other people are perfect because that place doesn't exist. Go somewhere you are willing to suffer and sacrifice when necessary—and it will be necessary—as you experience work for the rest of your life.

THE LOVE METRIC, PART I

If you've taken any type of survey in the last few years, you no doubt are familiar with the Net Promoter Score (NPS). Even if you've never heard of this system for customer feedback, I bet you'll recognize its signature question: "What is the likelihood that you would recommend Company X to a friend or colleague?"

That's a tough question to answer, isn't it? Very often, the real answers are "I don't know" and "It depends," and those don't fit neatly on a scale of 1 to 10. So unless things were awful or over-the-top wonderful, you might settle on some lukewarm score in the 4-to-7 range. When you think about what the question really asks, however, you end up with the significant conclusion that the NPS measures something greater than customer satisfaction. It measures the degree to which customers love the company.

Think of it as a "love metric," but it's not just a question we should ask of our customers. We all should be asking a similar question about ourselves, our lives, and the way we lead.

Let's make it a bit more direct and personal: Think about yourself. At the end of each part in this book, starting now, I'm going to challenge you to take the full measure of your business and personal life, including all your circumstances, relationships, and roles—coworker, businessperson, parent, friend, neighbor—and conduct an honest self-assessment.

Here's the first one:

To what degree are you doing what you love?

Rate yourself on a scale of 1 to 10, and then answer these questions:

Why did I give myself that score?

What score would people who know me give me if I asked them to rate me on that same question (to what degree do they think I'm doing what I love)?

What are three tangible things I can do in the next 30 days that would help me increase that score?

PART II

IN THE SERVICE OF PEOPLE

G reat! You're doing what you love. But as you may already suspect, this isn't only about you.

"In the service of people" is about the moral, ethical, and business context in which you're doing what you love. Yes, you're feeding your own heart, but are you serving others with the energy that you're creating by doing so?

This is the part that keeps you from devolving into a narcissistic tyrant who stomps on the hearts of employees and coworkers, swindles vendors and customers, and steals candy from babies— all just to get what you want in life. That's not you? Good, but it also prevents you from becoming a happy-go-lucky fool who is blind to the reality that people seldom *really* feel valued by your shallow, misguided attempts to make them feel loved. That's not you either? I believe you.

The truth is there are times when all of us bend in one of those directions. So let's explore what it means to bring a genuine outward focus to your leadership, your work, and your personal life—a moral and ethical context that guides you down the path as you do what you love.

6

GET OVER YOURSELF

Spread love everywhere you go; first of all in your house.
Give love to your children, to your wife or husband,
to a next-door neighbor. Let no one ever come to you
without leaving better and happier.
—MOTHER TERESA

THE BIG IDEA: DO WHAT YOU LOVE IN THE SERVICE OF PEOPLE

Maybe you've seen the photo floating around the Internet of a pack of wolves in a single-file line making their way across a snow-covered hillside in Canada's Wood Buffalo National Park. Chadden Hunter took the picture, and it was featured in *Frozen Planet*, a 2011 BBC documentary, but it didn't go viral on the Internet until a few years later when it became a popular metaphor about leadership.

The photo shows 25 timber wolves walking with gaps of separation between a few different groups. At the front, there are three wolves. According to the Internet metaphor, they are the oldest and the weakest of the pack, and they set the pace so that they won't get left behind. Next are five of the strongest members, and they provide protection from any frontal attack. The largest group is in the middle, and they are followed by another group of five of the strongest members who protects the pack's rear. Behind that group walks the lone alpha wolf, the leader of the pack. He ensures that no one is left behind and that the pack stays united as it moves along its path.

Researchers, of course, refute that theory. Some claim there's no such thing as an alpha wolf that dominates the pack (at least not in the wild). And most, including the photographer, claim the wolf at the front of this particular pack would have been one of the stronger members because that wolf needed to create the path through the thick snow.

I find the disagreement only makes the metaphor stronger. The fact is, it doesn't matter whether the leaders are in the front or the rear. What matters is the way they are leading the pack. In either case, the leaders are serving the other members. The leaders in the front are forging the path, providing direction, and making it easier for others to go where the pack needs to travel. The leaders in the rear are providing support. They are watching over the pack and, as the viral post suggests, ensuring that no one is left behind. There might even be some leaders in the middle of the pack because here's the thing about leaders: they serve others no matter where they find themselves.

This emphasis on service is the much-needed add-on to advice you hear all the time: "Follow your heart. Do what feels right. Do what you love." As we've outlined, Extreme Leadership begins with doing what you love. But it doesn't stop there. It can't stop there. You have to do what you love *in the service of people*. Not profits. Not status. Not a corner office. Not efficiency. Not market share.

People.

Again, there's nothing wrong with profits, status, a corner office, better efficiency, greater market share, or any other metric of business success. They are quite important. But if you *love* those things over people—if you put those things above the needs of the pack—then you'll end up causing more harm than good, even if you achieve some of your short-term goals.

Lone-wolf leadership only serves the lone wolf.

Extreme Leadership serves the pack.

Dan Cable, a professor at London Business School and author of *Alive at Work*, tells the story of a food delivery company whose goal-oriented approach backfired because it didn't serve the pack. The leadership team came up with a list of metrics to help reduce costs and improve delivery times by the drivers who took milk and bread into the UK marketplace. And their plan worked great . . . until they put it into practice.

"Each week, managers held weekly performance debriefs with drivers and went through a list of problems, complaints, and errors with a clipboard and pen," Cable wrote in an article for the *Harvard Business Review*. "This was not inspiring on any level, to either party. And, eventually, the drivers, many of whom had worked for the company for decades, became resentful."[1]

It wasn't that setting goals and holding people accountable were bad. It's just that they were conceived and executed with little regard for serving the people who were affected by them.

MORAL CONTEXT

If you do what you love but you love the wrong things, then you aren't serving others and you aren't practicing Extreme Leadership.

Think about it. You could argue that criminals do what they love. Some criminals might be effective leaders. They might motivate people. They might create a bold vision. They might develop a sound strategy. And they might achieve results. But something critical is missing from their leadership equation.

Or you could do what you love in perfectly legal and ethical ways but primarily to satisfy your selfish desires. Your work could be all about your goals, your business, your plans, your feelings, your success, your life—it could be all about you. There's a word that describes such leaders: *narcissists*. Something critical is missing from their leadership equation as well.

And what's missing, of course, is a sincere focus on serving the needs of others. That heartfelt focus provides the moral and ethical context that adds real value to doing what you love. Now you're not just feeding your ego when you do what you love. You're actually doing it to bring value to the lives of others. The motivation comes from the love of what you do—your work and your business—not because the employee handbook tells you to do it.

Consider, for example, Ethan Agarwal, an up-and-coming entrepreneur who is highly motivated by the ethical context when it comes to doing what he loves in the service of people who love what he does. This motivation was ingrained in him throughout his childhood in California. Because Ethan grew up as the son of an Indian-born college professor-turned-entrepreneur, he traveled the world from a young age. But he wasn't a toddler with a silver spoon in his mouth.

"If you go around the world in the late eighties, early nineties, which was when I was a kid, you see all kinds of things," he told me. "You see poverty that you don't run into on a daily basis in the United States, and you develop an empathy I think, which sticks with you throughout your adulthood."

Ethan began his professional career in investment banking, and he immediately made a practice of donating 10 percent of his salary to charity every year. As his career progressed, however, he realized he could do more, and not just give more money. He realized he could build a business that served the greater good.

Ethan's big idea was sparked, oddly enough, by the fact that he had gained about 40 unwanted pounds during graduate school. He was determined to get in better shape, but his travel schedule for work made it difficult to use a personal trainer while on the road, and scheduling time with a trainer was challenging when he was home in New York. Despite these challenges, he was able to lose the weight. But here's what really gnawed at him—unlike most people in the world, even many in America, he lived in a city with plenty of high-quality fitness centers and trainers, and he had the money to access it.

"Because of financial or geographic limitations, the perception of training had become that it was only for the elite," he told me. "You know—pro athletes, the überwealthy, celebrities; it was just for them. And when it comes to people's health, that doesn't feel right to me. It shouldn't be based on how rich you are or where you live."

So in 2016 Ethan started Aaptiv, a company that offers app-delivered personal training programs. Members have access to more than 2,500 guided workouts with trainers providing step-by-step audio instructions and popular music available to listen to while working out. Which they can do in the gym, at home, in the park—pretty much wherever they want. And at a reasonable price.

"No one was creating a product of high caliber but also at a price point that was accessible," Ethan said. "The analytical components said to me that there's clearly a market opportunity, but the reason I got really excited about it is because of the second point, which is that, it was just a moral opportunity."

When Ethan and I spoke near the end of 2018, Aaptiv employed around a hundred people in its offices at the World Trade Center. It had grown from 2,000 paying subscribers in 2016 to 250,000 by the end of 2018.

"To provide this product to millions of people around the world, we have to build a sustainable business model," he said. "It's not like we're money-hungry capitalists, but we're also not capable of building a great product if we don't care about money. If we just give it away for free and we have no standards, that wouldn't work either. So in the world where the mission of the company is to create a great product and get it in front of as many people as possible and help millions of people with their health, we have to do that with a business mind."

When you do what you love in the service of people, then what you do takes on a higher purpose—helping them succeed at what matters to them, helping them reach their potential, helping them overcome their challenges, helping them improve their quality of life, helping them find joy and contentment.

That's how you change the world.

I know this guy, by the way, who hates it when an author or speaker talks about how you, as a leader, can change the world. It just seems like way too much hyperbole to this guy. I get it. And I admit that "change the world" has become an overused cliché. It's much easier to talk about it than it is to do something about it.

But let me tell you this: if you want to change the world—*really* change the world—then all you have to do is add value to the lives of the people in your sphere of influence. That's it. Serve others. Because when you add value to their lives, their world will be a better place. It will change for the better.

THE PEOPLE YOU SERVE

Extreme Leaders always serve multiple constituencies: employees, peers, supervisors, stockholders, vendors, customers, clients, community members—the list goes on.

Most fit into two categories: the people inside your organization and the people your organization serves. (I started to call them *internal stakeholders* and *external stakeholders*, but those terms seem a little sterile, a little non-people-friendly.) Either way, the first order of business when it comes to serving these people is to get to know them.

If you don't know them, sometimes your most well-intentioned attempts at service can miss the mark. I know of an elementary school principal, for instance, who came away from a leadership training inspired to serve her teachers and staff by giving them "regular praise." She found opportunity after opportunity to tell them they were the greatest team in the history of education. But that team never really felt loved. Why? Because when they sent the principal an e-mail with a request, it disappeared into a black hole and was never answered. And when the principal had an idea for a new program or policy, she just rolled it out without ever seeking input from those who would have to live with it.

This principal would say she loves what she does and that she does it in the service of others—the students, teachers, staff, parents, and community. But clearly there's a disconnect: she doesn't really know the people she's serving well enough to serve them really well.

We established earlier that the type of love we're talking about in this book isn't romantic love. But even romantic love often doesn't start off as romantic love. It takes time to build that type of intimacy. And that time, often referred to as "dating," involves serving the other person's needs. In that regard, it's similar to what I'm talking about when it comes to doing what you love in the service of people.

In *The Radical Leap*, I used the analogy of a first date with someone you were really crazy about. First, you really paid attention, didn't you? You hung on every word, you noticed every detail of what your date was wearing, what she ordered for dinner, what songs he said he loved. And you took volumes of mental notes. You gathered data. And what did you do with that data? You responded. You took actions. You delivered on your date's expressed desires, and you tried to infer the unarticulated needs and respond to those too.

Now, I argue that relationships in the world of business are won in analogous ways: by paying nearly obsessive attention to the needs, desires, hopes, and aspirations of your employees, your colleagues, and your customers—often in very sacrificial ways. By knowing not only when to stand firm on your own principles but also when to sacrifice some of your short-term needs to become more personally fulfilled in the long haul. And by proving through your own actions that you really mean it, and that you're not simply following the advice that you gleaned from the latest book you read or podcast you listened to.

To show love, you need to put some skin in the game and genuinely, sacrificially, and unconditionally serve others. When you do this, you inevitably find yourself in some uncomfortable places. You see something you know needs to be done in the service of others, but you won't want to do it. Doing it is risky. Scary. In other words, you are experiencing an OS!M, and you need to act on it. If the thought of loving the people you work with scares you, that is an indicator that you're moving in the right direction, not an indicator that you need to avoid it.

Think of it for a moment from the standpoint of a follower. You are not going to follow just anybody into an uncertain future. You are not going to follow just anybody into a potentially threatening situation. You are not going to follow just anybody for a cause unless you love something about those leaders, if not the leaders themselves. And what is it you love? You love their ideals. You love their principles. You love their conviction. You love their vision and purpose. You love the way that they approach things. You love their energy. You love the way they care about the people around them.

In short, you love that the leaders are doing what they love and doing it in the service of others, including you.

Ethan Agarwal learned this principle from his father, Vinod Agarwal, who was, and still is, one of his mentors as an entrepreneur.

"The most important thing he said to me was to take care of your team and everything else will sort itself out," Ethan said. "He preaches that every day, and I think that's why he's been so successful in the companies that he's built—people love to work with him."

One of the ways Ethan takes care of his folks is by always making himself the lowest-paid member of the executive team.

"I'm asking everyone to invest in me, invest in themselves, and believe in the mission, so it's not right for me to siphon off capital from this company while we're trying to build it," he said. "There are lots of risks with startups, and lots of things that you have to figure out. So I try to reflect that by not compensating myself the most."

He also takes care of his team by hiring quality people who share the company's values. In fact, during one phase of the company's growth, he let one employee veto the hiring of a new manager who would have brought much-needed skills to the table. Why the veto? The employee felt the new guy wasn't a good fit. Specifically, she said she would be *less excited to come to work every day* knowing he was there.

That doesn't mean you serve employees by giving them what they want and making life easy on them.

"We have a very high-performance-driven culture," Ethan said. "I demand a lot from my team. We don't have a lot of patience for people who don't perform well. That is the culture. When people come here, they know that they're expected to work their butt off, to perform very well."

Those who don't embrace the culture don't stay.

"Look, I hate letting people go," he said. "It's one of the worst things, in fact, it is *the* worst thing, I have to do in this job. The way I always justify it to myself is that there are 99 other people, plus their families, who are relying on the performance of this business. If 2 or 3 people are hindering the performance of the business, then I'm not being fair to the other 99 people if we keep them around."

OUTSIDE YOUR WALLS

The other broad group of people you serve are those who live and work primarily outside the walls of your organization, otherwise known as "the rest of the world." Extreme Leaders don't just do what they love in the service of their employees and coworkers.

They also serve their vendors, their outside partners, their communities, their shareholders, and, of course, their customers and clients.

Obviously, no discussion about business makes any sense at all unless we bring the customer into it. Loving the customer, however, is very easy to talk about and very difficult to do. Every organization finds some way, formal or informal, to say, "We love our customers." And none of them post a banner on their website that says, "The customer is stupid. We wish they would get out of our way so we can get our jobs done around here." That's the way many of them act, but they all talk about the customer as being all-important and the very reason for their existence.

Now, I have had a lot of experiences—and I know you have too—with companies that talk the right game but drop the ball as far as action goes.

How many times have you been thrown platitudes like, "Have a nice day!" and "Thanks for flying with us!" Those are easy to say, but your experience—positive or negative—hinges on what they did to demonstrate that they really cared about your day or if they were truly thankful that you were on their flight.

The act of delivering love to a customer (or anyone, for that matter) is very personal. It is a personal connection. It is not simply about the language we use but also about our point of view and our mindset. And it is very, very clear to customers when a service provider is faking it or, worse, just doesn't care one whit.

Customers are savvier than ever, which means they (we) can be a skeptical and sometimes even cynical bunch, especially when it comes to corporate platitudes. I get e-mails, for instance, from an online retailer that often has this in the subject line: "☺ We thought of you the moment we saw these items!"

"Really?" I think to myself. "You saw hemorrhoid cushions and immediately thought of me?"

The thing is, many companies believe that if they come up with a snappy slogan and make their employees regurgitate it (in person or in e-mails), even their underachievers will charm the money out of customers. But far too often their training procedure sounds something like, "OK, slime balls, go out there and talk nice-nice to the customers—and remember that we love them."

This goes back to doing what you love in the service of the people who work with you or for you. If the leaders within a company talk about how important customers are but treat their own employees like dirt, the company is only fooling itself. On the other hand, if you are serving your employees with love, they will more likely reflect that same service of love with their customers.

Many platitudes are, in fact, excellent advice and inspiring mantras. But the companies with people who take these platitudes to heart are the ones we enjoy doing business with. They understand the value of another platitude: "You can't replace attitude with platitude." Don't bother with slogans unless you really mean them. Don't just *tell me* you love me. *Show me* you love me. Close the gap between *talking* about customer love and the actual behaviors that *demonstrate* customer love. Make me feel happy to be there. Make it a nice day. Don't just tell me I am worth any amount of money. Treat me that way. I will pay more. I guarantee it.

Ethan models customer love by creating a product his customers love. He can talk all day about the price point that meets customers' needs or the variety of training programs his company offers or the music that's available or any of the benefits his company has created for customers. But for Ethan, the proof is in the video testimonials their customers share with him—like the woman who was stationed at an army base in South Korea and used Aaptiv to get back in shape after having a baby, or the man who lost 200 pounds and not only felt better physically but saw improvements in his business because he was healthier emotionally.

ANTICAPITULATION LEADERSHIP

By the way, the customer is *not* always right. There's a difference between lovingly serving the customers' needs and always giving customers exactly what they say they want. Sometimes customers don't know what they need or want. In fact, sometimes what they need or want is very different from what they say they want or need. Companies like Apple, for instance, have made an art form out of figuring out what we, the customers, *really* want well before we have any clue that we want it. Before we know it, that thing we never imagined we would want has become that thing we can't live without.

Customers also are prone to want things that they not only don't need but that are not really good for them.

Movement Mortgage, for instance, was launched in 2008 during the recession because its founders believed the industry wasn't "loving the borrowers" by providing loans to people who clearly couldn't afford them. Their process begins with helping customers understand what they actually can afford.

Furthermore, sometimes giving customers what they want will put you out of business if you give it to them, which means you are no longer around to give them what they need. Several years ago, for example, Kirk Thompson, then CEO of the trucking and logistics company J.B. Hunt Transport, decided to create a new pricing structure that significantly raised its rates. The company had become a market leader because of the size of its trucking fleet, its commitment to excellent customer service, and its dependability, but low-cost competitors were turning its services into commodities. J.B. Hunt recognized that it couldn't survive much longer without raising its rates or lowering its quality.

The new pricing structure initially cost the company some business, but J.B. Hunt was up front with its customers about why it needed the change. And because other low-cost carriers weren't able to deliver as promised, most of the customers who left eventually came back and willingly paid for the real value of the services.[2]

Here's the point: whether we're serving our customers or our employees, love always looks like *value*. And value can take many forms. It might look like a Ping-Pong table in the break room, but it also might look like a difficult conversation about the result of missing a key deadline. It might look like suits that actually fit, or it might look like mortgages the customers can afford rather than putting them in a nice house but landing them in financial misery. And that's the key.

What does love in the service of people look like? Let's explore more examples.

7

PICTURES OF SERVICE

The purpose of life is not to be happy—but to matter,
to be productive, to be useful, to have it
make some difference that you lived at all.
—LEO ROSTEN

THE ENERGY,
AUDACITY, AND PROOF

What does it look like to serve people when you do what
you love?

We've all been on the receiving end of bad service, but some
people do get it right. Some really do care about our experiences
with their businesses, whether we are a coworker, an employee, or
a customer. They often seem like a rare breed, unfortunately, and
sometimes you have to travel great distances to find them. But if
you seek, you will find.

As you may have already gathered, I am a bit of a customer
service spy. I have worked with organizations over the years to
improve their customer practices, and I am always on the look-
out for examples of the great and the terrible in the fine art of
customer love.

One year when my kids were wee ones, I took my family on an international reconnaissance mission to the United Kingdom. I wanted to explore the Brits' effectiveness at dealing with the ultimate customer service challenge: me and my offspring. Also, I wanted a good excuse to write off our trip.

The British, I discovered, don't engage in the practice we call "customer service." They deliver what they call "customer care." That term alone should tell you something about the British approach to business. They don't just serve you. They care for you, which is really what happens when you do what you love in the service of people—you care for them. It is an emotional investment in the other person. *Care*, in this context, is defined as "to feel love or a liking for." And if *Webster's* equates care with love, that's good enough for me.

This idea of caring sounds contrary to the aloof and stuffy British stereotype. But in every British grocery store, restaurant, and castle that we patronized, we felt that the workers cared about us even when we inadvertently came off as the classic ugly Americans.

I remember standing at a cash register with my three children, and a growing line—sorry, *queue*—of Brits began fidgeting behind us like the entire Royal Guard waiting for the loo after tea time. I was frantically trying to figure out the coins in my hand—to read my pence, as it were—and in this fit of frustration, I thrust a fistful of currency at the cashier.

"Pick whatever works," I said.

The kindly queen's subject looked back at me with a tender smile. "That's all right, love," she said. "You'll get used to it, you will."

This was not your classic American behavior, right? I mean, in some cities, the clerk would have told me to go back to my own damn country if I couldn't figure out the currency.

It was this way throughout our trip. I was inspired by our British hosts, and I think that they can teach us a lesson about serving everyone who is connected to our business. We need to realize that service is not servitude; it is not menial labor. To care for people, no matter how difficult or impolite they may be at times, is, in fact, a way of life for all of us, whether we realize it or not. We all care for somebody. We care for clients, for family, for community, for friends. And by doing so more consistently and more intentionally, we can, even if only in small ways, have a positive impact on one another's lives.

When we do what we love in the service of people, those people feel cared for and valued—because they *are* cared for and valued. This isn't have-a-nice-day customer service or surface-level compliments during staff meetings. I'm talking about service that communicates a much deeper message, one that says, "I genuinely care for you as a human being. I want you to feel loved and valued and to have the resources you need for success." That level of love-based service creates stronger employee engagement and better customer service, which lead to good business results.

I understand, of course, that this level of personal investment into the lives of our coworkers, employees, customers, and clients can make you feel uncomfortable. It can seem out of place in many business environments. But as a top-notch customer care representative once told me, "That's all right, love. You'll get used to it, you will."

CHRIS VAN GORDER, SCRIPPS HEALTH

In 1978, Chris Van Gorder was a police officer in California when he was injured while responding to a domestic dispute. The injuries were so severe, in fact, that he spent weeks in and out of the hospital. He couldn't return to active duty, and he became so depressed that he began seeing a physician.

"He wrote me a prescription for some medication because he thought I was depressed," Van Gorder told me. "I walked out of the office and I remember thinking to myself, 'Shame on me. I'm feeling sorry for myself, and I've got to stop doing that.' I ripped up the prescription, and I made the decision at that point to rebuild my life and rebuild my body."

And that's exactly what he did.

Van Gorder ended up with a job as director of security and safety for the hospital where he had been treated, and that launched him on a new career path in the healthcare industry. Van Gorder worked his way through graduate school, got into hospital administration, and quickly rose to the executive ranks. He joined Scripps Health in San Diego in 1999 and became CEO in 2000.

"There are points in life when you can fall down or you can fall up," he said.

He chose to fall up, and now he tries to create a culture that helps others fall up as well.

The Scripps health system was losing about $15 million a year when he took over, but it soon became the only double-A-rated, tax-exempt healthcare system in California. It's highly rated for patient and employee satisfaction, and it's a regular on *Fortune*'s "100 Best Companies to Work For" list.

Van Gorder changed the culture and the business by serving the 15,000 employees and 2,600 affiliated physicians. Inspired by a trip to Haiti in the aftermath of the 2010 earthquake that devastated that country, Van Gorder committed the hospital system to a more horizontal structure that emphasized listening to staff and physicians and giving them more say-so in the policies and pro-grams of the company.

When he first became CEO, Van Gorder began meeting with frontline employees for Q&A sessions. Those meetings helped in-spire the Scripps Leadership Academy, a yearlong program for 25 managers at a time. When he decided to change the organi-zational structure after the trip to Haiti, he gathered the alumni from the leadership academy for a full-day retreat. He explained what he was proposing, why he was proposing it, how it would affect them, and why it wouldn't succeed without their support. Their buy-in, he said, was critical, and he only got it because he involved them in the process.

Van Gorder also set up a Physicians Leadership Cabinet, an advisory board that has access to information and data about key decisions for the entire organization. As they began to see the big picture, he told me, "they moved away from *what's good for me* to *what's good for the group*. It's been incredibly powerful."

Serving others, of course, also involved responding with love to needs that weren't part of the structure plan. When a manager and his daughter were injured by a grizzly bear attack while they were hiking in Washington's Glacier National Park, Van Gorder and his chief medical officer rushed to assist in their care. Later, they created what he called an "employee concierge"—one em-ployee who would look out for others during a crisis—and the Hope Fund, an employee-sponsored fund to help coworkers in need.

"You could argue it is good business to take care of your em-ployees," Van Gorder said, "but I think we've gone beyond that. This is an organization that already has passion because we're caregivers. If we don't love our people, they're not going to be able to love our patients. I think the whole culture of this organization is one of taking care of each other. Maybe 'love' is too strong of an expression, but I don't think it's an inappropriate one."

JOHN BALLENTINE, TANGO PRESS

If you work for John Ballentine, it won't be long before you hear three words that many employees around the world never hear from their boss: *I love you.*

Ballentine is cofounder of Tango Press, a digital print shop that mostly handles small-run orders of cardboard boxes used for product packaging or display cases. He's not shy about including love as an active part of his business and his leadership. In fact, if you work anywhere around Ballentine for long enough—even if you don't work for him—then there's a good chance you'll hear those words. Why? Because John Ballentine actually loves you, and he'll work hard to get to know you well enough that he can tell you that you are loved.

That's Ballentine's approach to life, and it has served him well in business, both with his customers and with his employees. His commitment to this approach began several years ago when he was a frustrated salesman working for International Paper. He'd been there less than five years and was struggling to feel like he had the trust of his boss. After a long period of literally spending hours on his knees in prayer, he said he felt a conviction to simply "bloom where you're planted" by proactively showing love to his coworkers and clients.

"I started digging into people's lives, figuring out how I could care for them, respecting them, building trust, just loving people wherever they were," he said. "It changed my whole attitude. And it changed my business. I went from selling $2 to $3 million to $26 million."

The financial returns were amazing, but his motivation was simply to show love and then trust that something good would come of it—for others, not for himself.

As he has progressed in his career, putting love at the center of his work has never failed him. It even rescued him on at least one occasion by allowing him to turn a mistake into a long-term positive. Ballentine made the mistake, he said, when he didn't push back against a directive. Ballentine worked for a team that was competing with another internal group to land a client, and he was told to go directly to the customer—and around his coworker in the other internal group—with a lower price. He did, and, of course, it infuriated his coworker in the other group.

"Eric was mad," Ballentine said of his coworker, "and it escalated throughout the company."

It also escalated the anxiety deep within Ballentine's soul.

"I thought long and hard about how I could make that right, about restoration," Ballentine said. "I swallowed my pride, went to Eric, and I told him I was sorry for what I had done. I didn't say anything about my directive from management. I asked for forgiveness and told him it would never happen again. We worked together some more after that and had some success. It took a while, but we rebuilt that trust."

In fact, six years later, after Eric had left that company and Ballentine had cofounded Tango Press, Ballentine got a call out of the blue from Eric.

"I need your help with a project," Eric said "Our customer is not happy with what we are doing."

The result was a long-running contract for Tango Press as a subcontractor for printing specialized boxes for a major tool manufacturer. Clearly, Ballentine's overall pattern of practicing love as a business principle earned him the respect of someone he had once hurt, not to mention additional business.

Ballentine's greatest enthusiasm when it comes to the value of serving others with love in his business is much more about the impact it has on people's lives rather than the return it provides to his bottom line. He sees this in his relationships with his customers, but the most powerful example involves one of his employees.

Ballentine needed a package designer, which is a pretty specialized skill in his industry. Fortunately, a friend knew someone. Charles Jennings was retired, but the friend said he might be willing to work a few hours a week. After a few failed attempts, Ballentine eventually contacted Jennings and invited him to come see their shop. Jennings showed up one day looking a bit frail as he hobbled in using a cane. After looking around, Jennings's face began to light up. "This is a package maker's playground," he said. Then he mentioned that he had wrecked his pickup, so a part-time job would be a good way to help pay for his new truck. Now Jennings is a key part of the team at Tango Press. He has his new truck, he no longer hobbles around with a cane, and he's always got a great attitude about his work.

One day, Ballentine was visiting with Jennings when he felt compelled to tell him how thankful he was for all that Jennings had added to their operations.

"I just want you to know I love you," Ballentine said as he finished his speech.

Jennings looked at him with tears in his eyes.

"John, you saved my life," he said. "I was sitting at home rotting. You gave me purpose again."

LONNIE GOLDEN,
PENN STATE UNIVERSITY

One of the most important gifts we give the people we love is the gift of trust. When we give trust, people feel respected and cared for—they feel like our love for them is somehow contributing to a higher quality of life.

There's an organizational component to serving people we love by giving them our trust. As Extreme Leaders, we need to look at the organization and the way it's structured—the systems, policies, procedures—that allow that trust to happen more readily with people.

Lonnie Golden, my friend since we were smart-ass kids at summer camp, researched the relationship between work hours and happiness. Golden is a professor at Penn State, and he is one of those rare labor economists who thinks about happiness at work. His research reveals that your work-related happiness (or "utility," to use the academic lingo) in large part boils down to having more control over your work hours.[1] Money matters, of course, but only to a point.

"When your income is really low," Golden told me, "it's amazing what doubling your income does for your well-being. But if you're already making a million dollars, making another million isn't going to double your utility. It still adds to your utility, but by much less than for someone who started with very little."

Control of your time, on the other hand, is always a big deal. Golden and his research colleagues (Julia Henly and Susan Lambert) have found a strong connection between happiness and the freedom to manage your work time to fit your needs. Since happy workers are productive workers, one way we can serve the employees we love is by trusting those employees to come and go as they please.

What does this look like? Well, it depends on the needs of the people involved. For some, it might be allowing them to work from home two days a week. Others might need to work a split shift so they can get their kids to and from school. Or they might need to work fewer hours during a particular phase in life. Or have Thursday afternoons off to go watch their kid play soccer.

Golden told me that flextime is both a productivity tool and a reward. It's typically a reward for the highest-performing employees, but it also can enhance performance. Granting employees greater control of their schedules might not make everyone more productive for every hour of every day, but it fosters an atmosphere of gratitude and trust that typically leads to productivity.

It also helps build a culture of reciprocal trust. When you say, in essence, "I trust you to get the job done," you tangibly and dramatically demonstrate how much you trust someone to be responsible, and you're much more likely to see that trust returned to you. When people feel happy and feel trusted, they are far more likely to stick around and work with passion.

I have a friend who works for Google (a "Googler," as they call themselves). It's very much a performance-based culture, but he has full control over his work schedule. He thrives in that system. He's happy and productive, and he has no interest in going anywhere else. The bigger challenge often is keeping people like him balanced so they aren't working too many hours.

If this all sounds too pie-in-the-sky, remember, giving employees more control of their schedules usually is a matter of creating a culture in which people feel comfortable asking for the schedule that's best for them.

Flextime isn't practical for everyone in every industry, of course, but it's not as impossible as some like to think. And offering some level of control can ultimately pay huge productivity dividends. The key is to listen to the people you love and then to serve them by being audacious enough to figure out a solution to their challenges.

MARY MILLER,
JANCOA JANITORIAL SERVICES

Tony and Mary Miller owned their own business in Cincinnati, Ohio, but the business, they will tell you, really owned them. They had a blended family with five children, and their quality of life was taking a hit as they poured hours and hours into their stagnant cleaning company.

"That was why we hired a consultant," Mary told me. "We knew there had to be a better way to build our business. We were stuck in the status quo."

The consultant quickly diagnosed the issue: Tony and Mary had a "people" problem. And until they solved that, he said, he couldn't help them build their business.

"Tony and I were out vacuuming all night last night," he told them. "We were supposed to be reviewing your systems and how you do things. I was pushing a vacuum, and that's not what you hired me for. Call me back someday when you get your people problem figured out."

The people on the Millers' team at JANCOA Janitorial Services weren't the problem. The problem was that they didn't have enough of those people to grow their company.

How did they solve that problem? By doing a better job of serving the people they had.

In the janitorial industry, employee turnover averages 380 to 400 percent a year, but the Millers reduced that to under 100 percent and grew JANCOA from 65 employees to more than 550. The key to employee retention, they discovered, rested in how effective the company was in improving the quality of life for its people.

Shortly after they were fired by the consultant, Tony and Mary took a hard look at their people problem. Among other things, they realized their employees had a tough time getting to and from work. So they bought a 15-passenger van, and Tony began driving the company's new shuttle service.

This provided a practical solution to one of their issues, but it also gave Tony an unexpected window into the lives of their employees. As the driver, he became an invisible presence at the wheel with an ear for all of the problems their employees had in life. And as he shared what he was hearing with his wife, the couple shifted their priorities and began building the company with more of an intentional focus on serving the needs of their employees.

"We realized we've got a real responsibility as owners of this company," Mary told me. "If we are hiring people, we can do the best we can to make their lives better."

That included connecting employees to programs that helped them become first-time homeowners, sponsoring literacy and language programs, and actively helping them identify their passions so they could identify their dream job—and then help them land it.

"We realized nobody dreams of being a janitor," Mary said. "We said, 'Come work for us. Give us your best three to five years.

We'll help make the connections you need to improve your quality of life.'"

People still left, but now they were leaving to pursue their passions, not to escape their pain. That meant fewer people were taking out the frustrations of their pain while they were at work. Instead, they worked energetically with an eye toward a brighter future. They were more self-aware and happier in their work, which meant they complained less, were more efficient, and did better work. JANCOA operated more efficiently, more consistently, and more profitably.

Many of the people who thought they would leave within five years ended up staying because they discovered they enjoyed what they were doing and appreciated the company. Others left only to return because they realized they missed the work environment they had left behind. And whether they left or stayed, they all helped recruit new employees. Mary actually ran the numbers one year and found that 57 percent of her employees were recruited by other employees. Another 17 percent came because of the recommendation of former employees.

JANCOA doubled its revenues in one four-year span, even though it didn't have a sales team. That's an indication that their employees were doing a good job and that their reputation was spreading organically. The same word of mouth that helped fill their employee pipeline also helped grow their customer base.

"Our customers love that they don't have different people in their building every night cleaning because our retention is so much better," Mary said.

By serving their people, Mary and Tony served their customers and cleaned up in their market in the process. More important, the business that once owned them now was a business they loved.

"We really weren't doing what we loved," Mary said. "The love developed as we began to focus on taking care of our employees rather than on how clean are the toilets and floors."

DICK NETTELL,
BANK OF AMERICA

Early on in my consulting career, I met Dick Nettell, who is, to this day, one of the most inspiring, productive, and loving leaders I've ever encountered. An avid fisherman, he's now enjoying his retirement, but his leadership legacy lives on in the lives of the people he influenced during his storied career.

Nettell has a simple philosophy for leadership: if you grab people by the heart, he says, the head comes along for the ride.

"It's not only the right thing to do," Nettell told me. "It's smart business."

Did I mention that Nettell was a senior vice president for Bank of America? You know, a money guy? Bankers are stereotyped for their love of money, not their love of people. But Nettell gets it. He knows love is damn good business.

One of the many ways he has lived this out is by placing a high value on recognizing people for their work, which is a great way to serve the people we love. When you love the people around you, you are interested in their lives, which means you take the time to learn their stories, and you discover what really matters to them. Once you know that, you can tap into that knowledge and celebrate those people in extraordinarily powerful ways.

"When you really listen to people," he told me, "you can tell what motivates them. It's not a real difficult thing. If you really understand and you know something about the people who are part of your team, it enriches not only your life, but it enriches theirs."

Perhaps my favorite illustration of this from Nettell's career involves the promotion of one of his former direct reports to the position of senior vice president. The employee—her name was Charlene—had run a customer service center, and Nettell knew how hard she had worked to earn the promotion. For some, titles don't mean much. Mainly that's true of those who already have nice titles. For those working their way up, like Charlene, the title is a watershed achievement, and Nettell knew it.

So Nettell took the letter he had written recommending Charlene for the promotion and put it in a nice matte frame. Then he arranged to briefly close the call center so he could bring everyone together when he announced the promotion, and he presented the framed letter to Charlene. What really set this celebration apart, however, was how he went a step further and personalized the recognition to make it memorable.

With the help of Charlene's administrative assistant, Nettell tracked down about 25 people who had played some role in Charlene's success. When he announced the promotion, those people were waiting on a conference line. He put them on speakerphone one at a time and gave each a chance to say a few kind words about Charlene for everyone to hear.

"The way I set this up, it was kind of a poor man's version of *This Is Your Life*," Nettell said. "I had the admin give each one of them a number. I would call on No. 1 and say, 'Do you have something to say?' That person would say something about his or her relationship with Charlene. She would then have to guess who it was."

No. 25 on the list, the final one, was a bit hesitant at first. After a few seconds, however, the group heard an elderly voice say, "I just want everyone out there to know how proud I am of the little farm girl from North Dakota."

It was Charlene's mother.

"I'll remember those words until the day I die," Nettell said. "There wasn't a dry eye in the house. It didn't cost a dime, but it meant the world to her and everyone else who participated."

Recognition is an act of service that's essential to building strong relationships.

"People say they don't have the budget or they aren't allowed to do anything in their environment," he said. "Those are all excuses from people who just aren't willing to do the work to recognize people in a meaningful way. It doesn't have to cost anything."

JOE JAROS, MARCO'S PIZZA

Joe Jaros was a driver for Marco's Pizza, and he loved his customers so much that they literally asked for him by name.

Who does that? Who calls for a pie and requests it be delivered by a specific driver? More important, why would they ask for him? Because the love Joe Jaros had for his customers showed up in the service he provided.

Joe did much more than quickly deliver piping-hot pizzas and subs. He would arrive at a customer's home, and, as he walked up to the door, if he noticed, for example, that the light bulb on the porch was out, guess what he would do? He'd change the light bulb. Why? Because that's what you do when you love somebody. You help him or her out. I guarantee you nowhere in his job description did it say, "change customers' light bulbs."

And Joe was delivering pizzas in Ohio, where they have this thing called winter. Maybe you've heard of it. Winter in places like Ohio comes with snow that piles up everywhere, often in drifts of three feet or more. So Joe would shovel the walk.

Shovel the walk, deliver the pizza. Change the light bulb, deliver the pizza. That's why people asked for him. That's why the owner of his franchise made him a partner in the store. And that's why Joe, at last count, was the owner of six stores in the Marco's chain, which now has more than 900 locations in 35 states and four countries.

When he was delivering pizzas, there probably were times when he thought, "I'll be a delivery boy for the rest of my life." That didn't matter. He loved his customers, and he took care of them—not because he thought he'd someday be given the opportunity to own a Marco's store but because it was the right thing to do. That's what you do when you love somebody. And it just so happens that it's also really good business.

Now here's a little epilogue to that story. A little old lady living alone in Ohio once fell in her home. An ambulance took her to the hospital, where they fixed her up. But when they asked her whom they could call to take her home, she said she had no friends or family. This lovely lady lived virtually alone on the planet, and she knew only one phone number by heart—the number of her local Marco's Pizza. So the hospital staff called Marco's and explained what was going on. Without hesitation, they sent one of their folks to pick up this lady and take her home.

There was no pizza involved. Not even a salad. And you know what? The store that sent that driver to pick her up is one of the stores owned by Joe Jaros.

8

UPPING YOUR
SERVICE GAME

*The best use of your hands is always love. The best way to say you
love is always time. The best time to love is always now.*
—ANN VOSKAMP

NOW WHAT?

When you do what you love in the service of people, at least
one outcome is inevitable: you will regularly experience
OS!Ms.

If you aren't pushing through some internal fear to serve
people, then you are falling short of what leadership is meant to
achieve. You might be managing. You might be providing some
help and direction and perhaps some encouraging words. You
might be contributing in some positive ways toward the goals of
your organization. And if that's all you're after, then that's great.
But if you aspire to leadership, you need to up your game.

When you empower someone on your team, for example,
you should do it knowing full well that failure is a very real pos-
sibility. Otherwise, it's not empowerment. It's management, and
sometimes you need to manage. Leadership, on the other hand,

involves risk. It means you will have that moment where you think, "Oh, man, what am I doing? I really hope they don't screw this up because my butt is on the line." If the OS!M isn't part of that experience of empowering somebody, then you haven't pushed it to the point of growth.

When it comes to doing what you love in the service of people, there are all sorts of practical steps to take. They don't all include an OS!M, but they all lead you toward one or help you take a leap of faith that lands you in authentic Extreme Leadership. So we'll end this part, as we did the previous one, with some practical advice from me and others on how to serve others as you do what you love (and some challenges to actually do it).

SERVE THEM WITH YOUR PRESENCE

It's not impossible to serve someone you don't know, but the more deeply you know someone, the more equipped you are to truly serve them. It's kind of a no-brainer, really. If you love someone or something, you invest time in learning all about that person or that thing. Then you can meet that person or that thing's needs. But I'd also argue that if you don't love a particular person, it's probably because you don't know him or her well enough.

So get to know your business, your industry, your job, your customers, your potential customers, your employees, your suppliers, your peers, your supervisors, your community members—everyone in your sphere of influence. Then you can serve them in radical, loving ways that produce damn good business.

And how do you get to know them? There's a really complicated solution, so you might slow down your speed reading to take this in.

Talk to them.

This means the first way to serve people is to give them your presence. Just show up and be you while in the presence of others. If you hang around long enough, one of you is bound to start talking and the other is bound to respond. Next thing you know, the two of you are having an old-fashioned conversation, and you didn't even need Twitter, Facebook, or Snapchat to make it happen.

I guarantee that if you invest time every week spending time with people and really paying attention to them, you will discover attributes and qualities you didn't know were there. Then you will start to feel a sense of appreciation and warmth. And, ultimately, you will end up with some colleagues you can honestly say you love and genuinely want to serve.

Many senior executives, by the way, still don't get this. There is still a separation; the executives don't mingle with the people on the front line. And the bigger the organization, the more difficult it is for the CEO to have any face-to-face human interactions with people "further down the organization."

They remind me of Frank Shirley, the character played by Brian Doyle-Murray in the classic comedy *Christmas Vacation*. Mr. Shirley is the boss who can't be distracted by the "little people" like Clark W. Griswold (Chevy Chase). He interacts with Clark in a couple of scenes, and it's pretty clear that he sees Clark only as an annoyance. The plot thickens when Clark learns Mr. Shirley has replaced the normal monetary end-of-year bonus with a subscription to the "jelly of the month" club.

You remember Clark's response, right?

His yuletide frustrations boil over, and he tells his living room full of relatives that he'd like his boss brought over "from his happy holiday slumber over there on Melody Lane with all the other rich people," so he can look him in the eye and "tell him what a cheap, lying, no-good, rotten, four-flushing, low-life, snake-licking, dirt-eating, inbred, overstuffed, ignorant, blood-sucking, dog-kissing, brainless, . . ." person he is. I cut the list short, because, well, it gets a little edgy, and this is a PG book, despite the four-letter word in the title. But you get the point.

If you haven't seen it, that scene sets up the frantic finish, complete with a kidnapping, a SWAT team rescue, a sewer explosion that sends Santa into the Chicago skies, and the singing of the national anthem. A happy ending for all. Hollywood at its finest.

The parody of the Mr. Shirley character is funny not because we all know a Mr. Shirley but because so many of us know a somewhat-like-Mr.-Shirley person. And you don't learn to love people, much less serve them, if you are a somewhat-like-Mr.-Shirley person in your organization.

The best advice I can give to my senior executive clients—this is not revolutionary, and I didn't make this up—is that you have got to be there. It used to be called *management by walking around* (MBWA). I don't care what you call it, but the bottom line is that you cannot understand another human being or another human being's point of view unless you are there, unless you can talk to that person face-to-face and say, "Tell me about your life. Tell me what you think."

> **Challenge:** It is very simple. Invest time in getting to know the people you serve, especially the ones you don't understand or see as " problems" in your work life. Talk with them. Ask questions. Listen empathetically. You may even find yourself making a new friend or earning a new ally.

SERVE THEM WITH EMPATHY

When you get to know people, you see them differently. You see their flaws differently. You see their problems differently. You see their skills differently. You see their attitudes differently. You see everything about them differently.

Empathy is when you are able to understand how people feel deeply enough to actually share their feelings. When they hurt, you hurt. When they experience happiness, you share in that happiness. When they act like jerks, you . . . well, you see beyond the action and into the cause. You see their pain or their frustration, and you *get it*. You may not like it, but you get it. Then you address the pain or source of their frustration rather than just responding from your own pain or frustration.

Ann Voskamp, author of *The Broken Way*, put it this way: "Sometimes it helps in the moment to think: people aren't being difficult—they are having difficulty." That allows you to respond in ways that serve them, which, ultimately, serves you and the business.

> **Challenge:** Identify the people you serve who are experiencing difficulties. How can understanding those difficulties help you serve them more effectively? Create an action plan for serving them.

SERVE THEM WITH KIND WORDS

Getting to know people is foundational, but you have to tell them you love the work they're doing, the contribution they're making to your own life and work experience, the fact that they spend their money on your products, and whatever else it is about them that you've come to appreciate after you've taken the steps to get to know them.

Here's one very simple way to do this: write them a note.

This is something of a lost art form in our digital world, but that only makes it all the more powerful. For years, I've asked audiences how many of them have ever gotten a personal note from someone and how many of them still have such a note in their possession. My unscientific research tells me that nearly 100 percent of the population has gotten a note and that somewhere around 85 percent of them still have it somewhere in a file or in a box. In fact, it's not unusual for many to say they've had the note for at least 10 years.

How long did it take the person who wrote that note to write it? A couple of minutes, and that's if they were really being ambitious. Three minutes of effort for a return that lasts 10, 20, or 30 years. Not a bad investment, right?

I brought this up for discussion at a workshop once, and one of the table groups was a team of managers. One of them had gotten such a note from one of the others.

"Bob, remember that note that you wrote to me?" he said. "We were sitting on the airplane, and it was the trip from hell. I just wanted to go home, and I was really down in the dumps. You wrote me this note telling me what a great job I was doing, and you really lifted my spirits. It just made the difference for me. Remember that?"

"Nope," Bob said. "You sure that was me?"

"Oh, yeah," the other guy said. "I'm sure."

Then he reached into his wallet, pulled out the note, which was written in Bob's handwriting and autographed by Bob. This guy had been carrying that note with him for 10 years. It was fuel that he ran on day after day after day, and Bob didn't even remember it.

Carl English was a senior leader at Consumers Energy in Michigan, a client for whom I'd facilitated a lot of off-site meetings in my days at the Tom Peters Company. Once, at the end of a rather intensive, weeklong session, Carl approached me at the front of the room.

"I have something for your youngest son," he said. "I want him to know what you're doing for us."

Then he handed me this note, which he'd written on a couple of pages of yellow legal paper:

> To Steve's Son,
>
> I understand that you are curious about what your dad does when his job takes him away from home. I bet it is tough on you, sometimes, to have him away when you would like to have him home more than he is.
>
> As one of his students this past week, I thought you might like to know what he did to help me and others in the class that he taught. Your dad has a lot of valuable knowledge about how businesses work and how to make them work better. Even more importantly, he helps people make their lives better and happier, and he teaches all this in a fun way so that the time we spend with him in class is really enjoyable.
>
> I just wanted you to know that we really appreciate your sharing him this week, and if he is anywhere near as good or as fun as a father as he is as a teacher, you have got yourself one fine dad.
>
> Carl English, one of your dad's students.

I choked back the tears.

When I got home, I gave the note to my son, Jeremy, who was seven or eight at the time, and he kind of chuckled his way through it.

"I guess it didn't have quite the same impact on him as it did on me," I thought. But he got downright defiant when I tried to take the note so I could store it in my personal "cool stories" file. It was *his* note, he pointed out. We negotiated a little, and finally he came up with the idea of framing the note and keeping it in his room. That way he could keep it, and I wouldn't lose it. Even better than framing, as it turned out, the note was immortalized by my mentors Jim Kouzes and Barry Posner in their extraordinary book *Encouraging the Heart*.

So the note Carl wrote out of the goodness of his heart in a spontaneous moment on a cold winter day in Michigan is now immortalized in a book (two of them now), and it is fuel that I run on. It is fuel for me on those days when I just want to go home, but my travels are taking me to the other side of the country or halfway around the world. It is fuel for me and fuel for my now-grown son. He will be able to show that letter in this book to his grandkids.

I shared that story several times with people at Consumers Energy, and every time—and I am not exaggerating—at least one person in the group had also gotten a note from Carl. I discovered that this was something Carl had done for years and years and years. People treasured these Carl English notes, and he wrote them for a very simple reason: Carl loved his work, and he loved the people who worked with him. Carl, by the way, went on to become president and CEO of the gas division of Consumers Energy and, later, COO, and then vice chairman of American Electric

Power, before retiring and, like our friend, Dick Nettell, leaving an inspiring leadership legacy in his wake.

I promise that if you make it a practice to sit down and think about whom you really appreciate and then capture your thoughts, very specifically, in a personal note, and then actually give that note to the person, not only will it become fuel for that person to run on but it will be fuel for you, too. What you begin to realize is that you actually have the ability to stimulate that feeling of appreciation in your heart. It is just a matter of practice.

Challenge: Start right now. List five people you appreciate and, over the course of the next week, write each one a note and give it to him or her.

What other acts of kindness can you do to serve others around you? Many of them will emerge from things you learn when you get to know the specifics of people's lives, but they might look like this:

- Cleaning the coffee pot in the break room

- Volunteering to drive to the airport for the next business trip

- Supporting someone's favorite charity with a donation of time or money

- Introducing people who have common interests or who can help each other solve some challenge

SERVE THEM WITH
YOUR PUBLIC OS!MS

You've probably heard the old expression that more lessons in life are "caught than taught." It's one in a long line of platitudes about leading by example. And for the most part, it's true. So one way you can serve the people you love is by showing them what it looks like to face fears and take risks.

The OS!M is not only for your personal growth as a leader. It's also a tool you actively use that serves others. In other words, don't hide your OS!M under a bushel. Let it shine, let it shine, let it shine.

Going public with your OS!M sends a message that it's OK to be scared, OK to take risks, and OK to screw up.

Watch me. Watch how I screw up from time to time, and watch what I learn from it.

The truth is, you screw up every day, and everyone already knows it. But when you show that you can face your screw-ups, when you can publicly acknowledge that you crashed and burned, when you can, metaphorically speaking, show the scars you earned when you fell down the mountain, you will become something to others that's very key to your leadership—human.

People don't follow idealized icons of unattainable perfection. By allowing others to participate in that OS!M with you, by allowing them to see your failings as a human being, they feel a stronger connection with you, human to human, and at the same time, they learn the lesson that it's OK to make those same kinds of mistakes.

What if you work in a culture that doesn't support risk taking? What if you're afraid of committing what many organizations refer to as a *CLM—a career-limiting move*? If you truly aspire to lead, if you really want to change the nature of things, and you happen to work in a risk-averse company, then your obligation, in my opinion, is to take these kinds of risks and prove through your own public and visible OS!Ms that risk intolerance is synonymous with stupidity.

What better way to serve the people, business, and customers you love than by helping remove the stupidity from your organizational culture?

One of my former clients provides a great illustration of how embracing a very public OS!M can serve others. She was a manager at a technology company. One day she walked into a staff meeting and handed out vouchers good for $1,000 to each member of her team, around 15 people. They could use the vouchers on any books, educational material, or software that would be helpful in doing their jobs.

"You've got $1,000," she said. "Spend it any way you want as long as it is in this area." Furthermore, she said, "I am going to buy you all lunch as long as you have that lunch with somebody else from work and you are talking about work over lunch."

She didn't ask her boss or anybody in accounting or finance. She just took it out of her own budget and did it. Well, it took less than 24 hours for her to get a phone call from on high. It was someone in the accounting office with a simple question about her plan: "What the hell are you doing? These people are going to rob you blind."

"No, they won't," she said. "They will use it just the right way."

When she was passing out those vouchers, of course, she thought to herself, "I believe they will do the right thing, but man, oh, man, I also hope they won't take advantage of this and of me." In other words, it was an OS!M.

Well, a couple of weeks went by, and the team had spent a grand total of $300. She actually had to go back and encourage them to spend the money. If she hadn't been willing to scare herself in the process of giving unprecedented discretion to her team, they never would have had the chance to prove their good judgment and trustworthiness to their leader and, indeed, to the entire company. That's not empowerment as a buzzword. It's empowerment as an act of Extreme Leadership.

Challenge: Sometimes serving others is downright scary. Don't let that fear stop you. In fact, it should motivate you to action. As you consider ways to serve others, consider these questions:

- What OS!M have you experienced recently that no one knows about but you? How can you share that experience?

- What OS!M are you considering that would require vulnerability in front of the people around you?

- What's the perception in your organization when it comes to taking risks or challenging conventional thinking? What are some ways you can challenge the status quo with your own OS!Ms and thereby pave the road for others to do so as well?

SERVE THEM BY BEING A STRONG FRAME

Dance instructors often talk about the importance of providing a strong frame in a partnership. It means the leader is in control but not controlling, steady but not overwhelming. It means the follower can lean into the leader with confidence and that guidance—and correction—will come when it's required.

Leaders show love to the people around them by acting as a strong frame, especially when there's a need for guidance or correction.

I know a leader who had earned rock-star status at his company by running a new division as it grew from almost nothing to being the most profitable piece of the company's lineup. But the music died the day their biggest client canceled its contract, and this leader soon called his team together and asked for advice on how to regroup. They came back with namby-pamby suggestions like, "Fire your assistant" and "Stop flying on the company airplane." The leader went to his CEO for advice, and the CEO basically said this: "Stop asking them to do your job. They need you to give them a plan. Give them direction, and hold them accountable."

For him, the OS!M wasn't about asking for help and input— that was the easy way out. The OS!M was about taking charge when those around him needed him to take charge and holding people accountable for their work.

He went back and wrote out a list of what he thought each of his direct reports needed to do. Then he called them in one by one and told them what he expected done and when it needed to be done.

"If you don't want to do that," he said, "tender your resignation. I am not going down like this. We can fix this. But you're going to do it my way."

That might sound tough, but it was exactly what they needed— and wanted.

"They wanted me to lead them," he said. "They wanted me to give them direction. Once they found some purpose in that direction, they were able to take ownership of it."

That leader was John Roberts, who went on to succeed Kirk Thompson as CEO of J.B. Hunt Transport.[1]

There's a time to listen to the thoughts, concerns, and recommendations of your team, but Extreme Leaders also show love by setting the course, showing the way, and holding people accountable. You don't have to be a jerk to provide what's often labeled as "tough love." But if you don't provide that aspect of a strong frame, you really aren't serving the people you love.

> **Challenge:** How do you handle the tough conversations you must have as a leader? The conversations that require you to prod people toward places they may not want to go or correct people when they've gone off course?
>
> Start by identifying a difficult conversation you need to have and then commit to having it—in the spirit of love and service.

SERVE THEM BY CREATING SHARED VALUES

We talked a lot about values when we were discussing how to do what you love. So when it comes to doing what you love in the service of others, it only makes sense that they know what you value and you know what they value. When you discover how and where those values align, you can serve each other in more meaningful ways.

I spent a few years working with the senior team of a medical manufacturing company in Silicon Valley. This was a team that had been working together for several years and knew each other pretty well. During an off-site workshop, I asked them to identify their values, post them on the wall, and tell some stories about them. We found some very significant common ground, but the one that each person on this executive team had listed as a key value was "family."

That might not sound like much of a surprise, and, in fact, every time I have done an exercise like this in just about any company, "family" or "balance" or "balancing family and work" comes up as a core value. But what was significant for this particular group of folks was that they didn't know that about each other. They discovered in that moment that they had been operating under the myth that work comes first and that you're expected to sacrifice some of the important things going on in your family life to get the work done.

After discovering that shared value, they looked at each other in a different light and said, "You mean all those times that I missed that important soccer playoff game and went to work instead, you would have supported me in staying home and you would have even filled in for me if that were necessary?" And that was the case.

The reality was that they weren't serving each other because they didn't recognize their shared values.

> **Challenge:** Get your team together and ask each individual, "What do you stand for? What are you willing to stick your neck out for?" Start this as an individual exercise, and then compare your notes as a group and look for the commonalities. What values do you all seem to share? You might express them in different words, but when you have a

discussion about what these values mean, then you will find that there typically will be three to six (maybe even more) that you all say are important.

Once you have made a commitment to each other to honor those values, regardless of what the values of the organization are, regardless of what it says on some laminated card, then you will have defined what is important about how you work together. What's more, getting clear on and articulating what is really important to you as a team means that when it comes time to take a stand as a leader, you are not doing it in the dark. You and every other leader on your team can take that stand on principle, which will help you (and them) push through the fears that come with an OS!M.

By aligning on your values, you are serving your team and empowering them to defend principles you all want represented in the organization. You are serving them by creating standards for accountability to what really matters to each of you.

SERVE THEM
WITH VALUABLE STUFF

When we do what we love in the service of people, those people end up getting something of value, and very often that something of value looks like stuff: great products and services that truly meet their needs (not just your needs), employee perks and benefits, or services to the community to raise everyone's quality of life.

Movement Mortgage, for instance, offers a number of initiatives that focus on "family and relationships, physical health and wellness, financial stability, and professional development." It also has a Love Works Fund. About 70 percent of its employees contribute to the fund, and the company matches those donations dollar for dollar. The fund helps employees out financially in times of crisis. And its Movement Foundation has invested more than $25 million in worthwhile community projects since 2008.

New York City–based recruiting service CloserIQ, meanwhile, provides its employees with benefits that exceed the norm, such as training opportunities, community events, happy hours, and reimbursements for gym memberships. Anything that makes them feel valued.

Those types of benefits have to come from the heart of the giver, and they have to touch the heart of the receiver. As a leader, you have to give something the other person really values, which may be obvious. But you also need to believe in and feel great about the gift you're giving.

> **Challenge:** Know your team and your customers, and then elevate their needs to a place of payable priority. That's where you're willing to shell out a little dough to let them see and feel how much you care.
>
> When you do that, they'll not only appreciate the benefit but also the fact that you knew them well enough to realize they'd appreciate it.

THE LOVE METRIC, PART II

At the end of Part I, I challenged you to rate yourself according to a love metric, my version of the Net Promoter Score (NPS). It's time to move to the next part of that assessment.

Once again, think about yourself and take the full measure of your business and personal life, including all your circumstances, relationships, and roles: coworker, businessperson, parent, friend, and neighbor. Now ask yourself this question:

> To what degree am I serving others?

Rate yourself on a scale of 1 to 10, and then answer these questions:

> Why did I give myself that score?

> What score would people who know me give me if I asked them to rate me on that same question (to what degree do they think I'm serving others)?

> What are three tangible things I can do in the next 30 days that would help me increase that score?

Now ask the people you're serving to answer the same questions about you. What are the gaps between how you see yourself and your service versus how others see you and your service to them? And what can you do to close those gaps?

PART III

WHO LOVE WHAT YOU DO

Here's the payoff for doing what you love in the service of others: they love you back—not just personally, but organizationally. Again, it starts with your team. If you lead with a passion for your work and your people and you serve them, they will love what you're doing and what they're doing. Then your customers will feel it and see it in your products and services, which means they will love it too.

The result is employee and customer loyalty, repeat business, low turnover, and high engagement. In other words, damn good business.

9

THE ROI OF LOVE

When we're nice to people, turns out, people are nice back.
P.S. The opposite is also true.
—SIMON SINEK

THE BIG IDEA: DO WHAT YOU LOVE
IN THE SERVICE OF PEOPLE
WHO LOVE WHAT YOU DO

Business leaders love acronyms. Maybe not as much as consultants, drill sergeants, or Baptist preachers, but it's close. And few acronyms are dearer to the hearts of business leaders than this one: ROI.

Ah, yes, the holy grail of all business acronyms—the return on investment. This, fellow laborers, is the payoff! It's the pot of gold at the end of the rainbow. You deposit your time, your money, your brain power, your strategies, your vision, your sleep, and anything else that you think might help, all in anticipation of seeing the return on that investment.

Infusing your business with love produces a return on your investment, and that return begins with another type of ROI—the *reciprocity on investment*. When you do what you love in the service of people, most of them will love what you do and give love right back to you and your business. Those who don't? Well, quite frankly, you don't need them. Keep loving them. But love them enough to help them find a different job or product that they really love. It's what's best for them, so they'll love you for it later. It's also what's best for you, and it's what's best for your business.

If you do what you love in the service of people who don't care diddly-squat about what you do, then you are, to put it mildly, wasting your time. Now, that's not always the case. As I said, we should never stop loving, and there's no quid pro quo involved when it comes to love. We should love our family members unconditionally. We should love our neighbors unconditionally. We should love our enemies unconditionally. Frankly, I'm convinced that unconditional love eventually produces a favorable return in any relationship, but I also know that sometimes "eventually" means years or even decades. We might not even live to see it.

What I'm talking about, however, is the focus of our love in business. We want people to love what we do. Some folks simply won't share our passion for the services or products we're offering. If we make products for dogs, we may not have a lot of cat lovers as employees or customers. They might not fight against us, but they probably won't love what we do. And that's fine.

Elay Cohen, the cofounder and CEO of SalesHood, runs a business that thrives on the idea of providing frank but constructive feedback that helps make sales teams better. Naturally, they value collaborative feedback as a culture. That includes tons of recognitions for what people do, he told me, but it also means providing the type of tough love that isn't always easy to take.

"Because we are very transparent and because we're giving feedback, it's not a culture for everyone," Cohen said. "Some people don't want the feedback. And we've had a couple people who have come in during their exit interviews and said we have a really tough culture. It's tough getting the feedback on a regular basis. And that's OK. That's not a regrettable departure."

But when we do what we love in the service of people *who love what we do*—clients, customers, coworkers, employees, and others—those people will reciprocate. This is great for at least two reasons. One, it provides proof that we are actually doing a good job of doing what we love in the service of people associated with our work. If they don't love what we do—and we'll rule out the jerks, malcontents, and people who simply don't share our interests—then it indicates we might have some blind spots or skill deficiencies. We need to get better at sharing our passions and serving our people. But if people actually love what we do, then there's a sense of validation. We're on the right track.

Two, when everyone in and around our organization is doing what they love in the service of people who love what they do, it creates *compound reciprocity on investment*. It's as if everyone put $10,000 into a joint mutual fund and watched their earnings multiply far more quickly than it would have on its own. Compound ROI leads to a return not just on your investments of love but every type of investment you've put into your work and your business: your time, your energy, your money, your dreams, your blood, your sweat, and your tears.

When the collective values, vision, purpose, and passions of a group align, momentum builds and magic ensues. And isn't this what more and more workers want—make that *demand*—in our modern world of business? Consider this quote from a best-selling book: "People want to work for a cause, not just a living. When there is alignment between the cause of the company and the cause of its people, move over, because there *will* be extraordinary performance!"

Sounds like something written about motivating the millennial generation, right? Actually, William Pollard, former chairman of ServiceMaster, wrote that in *The Soul of the Firm*, which was originally published in 1996.

Pollard's words were true then, they are true today, and they will be true forever. Viktor Frankl, in his seminal book *Man's Search for Meaning*, argued that the single greatest driving force in human beings is our desire to discover meaning. Not money, as Karl Marx claimed, or sex, as Sigmund Freud suggested. But meaning. That's not to say money and sex aren't strong motivators, but they aren't enough and never have been. The quest for purpose has always been important, but I don't think it's ever been more relevant than it is now. There's a growing hunger around the world for purpose and meaning in work, and the only way to feed it is by building companies with employees and customers who love what you do.

If you do what you love (your work and the purpose of the business), you're off to a great start. And if you do that in the service of those around you, then you've added the moral context. But when you create a sense of mutual love—a shared, reciprocal love for what you're doing—then you'll begin to see dramatic, impactful, life-changing returns unlike anything you've ever imagined.

VISIONS OF LOVE

As an Extreme Leader, you're regularly looking at the world around you and boldly proclaiming your message: *Follow me into the future!* You might not use those words, but that's your message.

Your followers, meanwhile, respond by blasting through whatever brick wall has been placed between them and accomplishing your vision.

Well, maybe that's not their first response.

Before they slam their sledgehammers into that metaphorical brick and mortar, they are rightly asking some questions, starting with, "Where are we going and why?"

Some might follow you out of blind loyalty or obligation to a paycheck, but those types of followers seldom produce consistent excellence or a passion that creates momentum. You want them to follow you with love, energy, audacity, and proof. You want them to leap with you into the future, regardless of the challenges they'll face along the way. They won't do that unless they love where you're going and why you're going there.

In traditional business-speak, they need to catch the vision or what's now often referred to as a "shared purpose." That's why countless business and leadership books talk about the importance of capturing that purpose in a formal corporate mantra— the mission, vision, and values statements. And that's why your organization no doubt has finely crafted, darn-near poetic mission and vision statements for all to read. Unfortunately, there is a significant gap between how effectively executives think they are communicating the corporate mantra and how well their constituents actually understand, remember, and embrace it. In short, most corporate statements are generic and meaningless to the very people they are supposed to inspire.

I believe this is largely because these statements are generally treated as a one-time event, whereas shared love for a vision and mission is a living, breathing, active part of a culture. The role of the leader is to make the vision meaningful. To give the mission life. To give the mantras a soul that others can love and, therefore, follow.

John Beeder is an executive who had been through more than his share of bad exercises crafting statements meant to capture the essence of a company, but he agreed to give it one more shot around 2010 when he was a senior vice president of American Greetings (AG), the Ohio-based card company that gives you a million clever ways to say get well, happy birthday, congratulations, and I'm sorry. A former executive at Walmart—one of the last remaining true protégés of Sam Walton—led the off-site meeting with about 20 members of John's leadership team. Eventually, they got to the crux of the matter with this question: "What do you want people to feel when they come to your company?"

"It was so interesting because you almost had a generational split," John, who served as AG's president and CEO before retiring in 2019, told me. "The younger executives, who were probably in their late thirties and early forties, described what they felt. The older executives were all hung up on hierarchical, theoretical types of management. They were into MBA verbiage and all that kind of stuff. I just dropped it. I probably didn't even think about it for six months."

Then something unexpected happened. The younger executives showed up in his office one day with a beautifully written statement describing what the company aspired to be. John loved what he saw—values that talked about creativity, innovation, collaboration, success, and people, and a vision that spoke of making "the world a more thoughtful and caring place." But to fully unite their culture behind a shared purpose, John also felt they needed a mission statement.

"We brainstormed for probably an hour," he said, "and they, not me—I had nothing to do with this—came up with the idea of getting Zev [Weiss] and Jeff [Weiss], the great-grandsons of the founder, to see if they could design a mission statement."

So John brought in Zev and Jeff, who at the time were co-CEOs. John showed them the vision and values statements and told them he was locking them in the conference room until they came up with a mission statement for the company that had been founded in 1906. About 20 minutes later, the brothers knocked on the door and told John their work was done.

"We create happiness, laughter, and love," they said.

John looked at them and said, "What the heck? Where did that come from?"

It turns out it was the first time they had been asked to think about it, but John knew it was perfect for the company.

"It captured the imagination of the associates," John said. "The customers said, 'I get it now.' If you talked to all of our constituencies, the entire 360 degrees, everybody got it. People integrated it into their daily business activities. I have people who just type 'HLL' on letters instead of saying, 'Sincerely.' It's really impressive, and it all came from some other entity pushing us a little bit."

From that, the company developed a purpose statement.

"If our mission is to create happiness, laughter, and love," John said, "our purpose is to make the world a more thoughtful and caring place. Now I've got a nice messaging hierarchy that I can apply to multiple things as we talk to people about who American Greeting is and what we do. For a lot of companies, that's really hard."

Branding everything with their purpose raised the bar for John and his management team. They have to make sure the company lives up to its promise of "happiness, laughter, love, thoughtfulness, and caring" in all that it does, from the cards it produces to the advertisements it creates to the healthcare benefits it provides. But as the leaders and everyone else began living out these cultural statements, something magical began to happen. Not only were employees more engaged and more productive but also the business improved in the form of higher profits and greater market share. Then the Weiss family decided to take it even further, and they announced they wanted to build a new 600,000-square-foot headquarters designed specifically to support the mission statement.

"We're going to lock this culture in," they told John.

The facility, known as the Creative Studios, opened in 2016 in the Cleveland suburb of Westlake, Ohio. The five-story building was designed, with input from the creatives who work there, so that natural light flows into all the work spaces. It has a town square, photo and audio studios, artist workshops, and a 10,000-volume reference library, and there's a coffee shop on every floor. There's even an outdoor park in the middle of the donut-shaped building—on the rooftop of the third floor. And the words "happiness, laughter, and love" are painted prominently on the building's lobby wall as a public declaration for everyone to see—employees and visitors alike.

"I didn't plan on building a new building," John said. "This thing just took off on its own. A little mission statement written in a room over lunch turned into something that basically cemented our culture for the next 40 or 50 years."

The creation of a shared-love mission and vision is that place where it all comes together—where the leaders' aspirations, hopes, dreams, and ideals all align with the aspirations, hopes, dreams, and ideals of the organization. That is where the inspiration is conceived. That is where the life is born. That is where the love is generated. But it's not found on a spot on a map. It's found all across the actual landscape. That is where the magic happens because that's where the shared love morphs and grows into a better version of itself with every passing tick of the clock.

Our goal as Extreme Leaders is to know ourselves, our companies, our businesses, our constituents, our colleagues, our co-workers, and our customers so well that we can not only articulate our shared vision—our shared love—but we can also embody what it is that we need to create together as we all do what we love in the service of people who love what we do.

That's all much easier said than done. We face resistance. We get tired. We get distracted. We lose focus. We don't just hit a few brick walls—we inevitably go into valleys that are filled with pea-soup-thick fog. And that's the paradox with vision: the harder it is to live it out authentically in the moment, the more important it is to the success of everyone involved. The deeper the fog gets, the more important it is to see. But it's hard to see in the dark.

NIGHT VISION

Carl Hammerschlag, who is both a psychiatrist and the author of *The Theft of the Spirit*, was right on the money when he wrote that "most of us scale down our dreams to the size of our fears until our vision becomes so tunneled we see darkness everywhere." A visionary, he said, is the "one who learns to see in the dark, not the one who describes it."

We have become very, very good at describing the darkness around us, particularly at work. If you have ever read *Dilbert*, for example, you know that Scott Adams is very, very good at describing the darkness around us. For 30 years, this cartoon has been the voice of corporate cynicism. He works in the extremes because that's how humor works best. But we relate to it because so much of it reflects the pieces of the realities we've experienced.

The talk around the water coolers often describes the darkness. The lunch discussions focus on the "idiot boss" we have to put up with or the "stupid decisions" that people are making. We can talk about that darkness all day long, and we can recount it again when we get home. But when it comes time to describe what kind of brightness we can create, what kind of future we can build together, we tend to freeze up. We are afraid to discuss it, much less do it.

We are afraid we are going to be wrong. We are afraid we are going to put a stake in the ground, and then the future will come to pass in a way that is entirely opposite from what we described. Then people will think we are stupid, incompetent, or both.

We are afraid to talk about the future we want to create because we believe people are going to judge us as overly optimistic or Pollyannaish. We can sense that they will be rolling their eyes when we're not looking, and maybe they are.

We clam up for lots of reasons, but a true visionary isn't afraid of the dark. The visionary looks into that scary abyss and sees what is good, even if it's hidden or not yet created.

The role of the Extreme Leader is not to deny the darkness. It's not to turn a blind eye to the problems and the challenges. It's just the opposite. The Extreme Leader acknowledges the challenges and then guides us into a meaningful, constructive conversation about how we can change things, about what the future can be like, and about how we can create it together.

That is the act of shared love. That is when vision becomes alive and powerful.

The best examples of compelling, inspiring shared-love visions are found by revisiting some of the darkest times in US history. Dial your DeLorean back to August 28, 1963. Go to the steps of the Lincoln Memorial, where, of course, you'll witness Dr. Martin

Luther King, Jr., speaking at a rally that was part of the civil rights movement.

If you had to quote Dr. King right now off the top of your head, what words would come to mind?

"I have a dream." Right?

That famous speech on that hot August day in 1963 has been referred to over and over, and it is used constantly as an example of an inspiring vision in a social context. Certainly, it is applicable in a business context, as well. It is applicable in the context of the human condition.

Do an analysis of that speech, and you will find that Dr. King talked in terms of the impact. He talked in terms of the images. He talked in terms of ideals. It was deeply rooted in his own passion and commitment. The power of that speech was in the shared love that came from the heart of an Extreme Leader. I guarantee you we would not be reciting that speech today if he had stood in front of those 250,000 people and said, "I have a list of measurable objectives. I can e-mail you the PowerPoint when I'm done."

Did he have measurable objectives? Yes. Did he have strategy? Yes. Did he have tactics? Yes. Did he have a plan, goals, and all that other stuff? Certainly. But he also understood that those were not particularly inspiring—not to himself, not to his supporters, and, most of all, not to people who had not yet bought into his vision.

You have to have the objectives and the plan, but really what inspires people is the potential to create something extraordinary together. And what happens all too often in business is that people really think they've identified the vision for the future when they have been very, very clear on the numbers that they have to hit.

Our vision is to become an x-million-dollar or x-billion-dollar or x tens of thousands of dollars company [or team, department, or project] within the next five years.

That's great. Numbers are important. What isn't measured, Peter Drucker famously preached, can't be managed. But that is not vision.

Vision answers questions like these: "When we hit those numbers, what is it going to be like around here?" "As we strive toward that goal, what kind of an impact are we going to have? How are our lives going to change?" "How are the lives of our customers going to change by virtue of what we do here?"

Progressing toward that number is what enables us to keep going toward that vision because obviously business is about making money. We don't want to deny that. But the vision is about getting very clear on the impact of that money and the impact of that success. That is what brings people to work every day.

A vision that really fills people up, draws them to work, keeps them engaged through difficult times, and keeps them in place through prosperous times needs to appeal to our hearts. That's where love comes in. If the vision creates and feeds on shared love, it will provide energy to get us through each day, it will cultivate audacious innovations, and it will be provable in small ways as we work toward the bigger goals.

TAPPING INTO YOUR INNER MADMAN

The poet Charles Bukowski said, "The difference between a madman and a professional is that a pro does as well as he can within what he has set out to do and a madman does exceptionally well at what he can't help doing."

I guess that makes me a madman. I can't help but do what I do because I love it. If that means I am nuts, that's fine. I can live with that. My work gives me energy and feeds an audacious belief that I can change the world. And I attempt to prove it every day of my life.

I believe my team and my clients feed off that love. When I share it in my actions, they catch the vision, and they join me in creating a future that's better than the present.

And I believe all leaders who do what they love in the service of people can tap into that love in ways that allow them to share it with others who also will love what they do. Getting it out of them, however, often involves an OS!M.

Peter Alduino, a colleague of mine from the Tom Peters Company, was working with a biotech company way back in the olden days of the 1990s. There was a big race going on at the time to identify and map all of the genes of the human genome, and this company was a part of this very competitive environment. Everyone involved felt an undeniable sense of urgency.

Peter was helping the senior scientist in this biotech company prepare for an off-site with his senior staff at which he would announce a reorganization. Well, you know how people love reorganizations, right? Like they love drinking sewage. Like they love standing barefoot on hot coals.

Here's the question Peter asked of this senior scientist: "Why do you care about this reorg? Why is it important to you?"

The answer he got was along these lines: "Well, you know, these are all scientists, and because they all report directly to me right now, I am spending most of my time solving their problems. That means I don't have the time I need to spend in Washington working with the broader scientific community. I am just putting out their fires all the time and losing sight of the bigger issues."

As answers go, that one was . . . well, it qualified as an answer. It was a knee-jerk answer. A surface-level answer. And it was not enough. Imagine if you were one of the scientists working for this guy, and he came to the off-site meeting and said, "OK, we're going to reorganize our team structure because, frankly, I am just spending way too much time on all your problems. I need more time to do what's important to me." How committed would you be to that reorganization? Not very, right?

So Peter, being the Socratic fellow that he is, didn't leave it there. He asked the question again.

"Why do you care about this? Why is this important to you?"

"Well, you know, because I am wasting a lot of time."

"That is not it. That is not the answer yet. Why do you care? Why does this matter? You say you are spending all this time on other people's problems and you are not involved in the broader scientific community. So what? What is the big deal? Why do you care about that, and why is that so important?"

On it went. The scientist kept dodging the question, and Peter kept asking. Finally, the top popped off the jar (or the beaker).

"I will tell you why I care," he said. "Because 500 years from now, the time that we live in right now is going to be remembered for two things. One, we developed the technology to save the human race, and, two, we developed the technology to destroy the human race. I want us to be remembered for developing the technology to save the human race. That is why this is important."

Now, if you heard that from your boss, are you more likely to enlist in this reorganization? Probably so. And, in fact, that's the way it turned out. His team bought in because, frankly, that's why they were all there. It was a shared vision. A shared love. That was why they loved their work. That was why it was worth it to put up with all the struggles. That was why it was worth it to put up with the tremendous pressure. That was why it was worth it to put up with the politics in the scientific community, in the company, and in the government. They really loved the cause they were pursuing.

When strategies, tactics, plans, goals, metrics, and all of those other necessary aspects of business planning tap into the shared love, then the people will be energized for progress. And the result is damn good business.

Why do you care about your business? I'll go out on a limb here and guess that you aren't saving the human race through biotechnology (if you are, God bless you for it). But you are doing something you love in the service of people, which means you are making a difference in the lives of others. You are changing your corner of the world, however big that corner might be. And because you are doing that, the people you are serving will appreciate it and share your love for it.

Tap into that passion and share that love.

SPREADING THE LOVE

In business, the *reciprocity on investment* that comes from doing what you love in the service of people who love what you do really takes off when it moves from your internal teams to your external constituents.

Don't get this out of order. You have to lead with love first and foremost, or else you won't create a culture of love within your organization. And you have to create a culture of love within your organization, or else you won't experience the reciprocity of love from those who do business with you.

That external group can come in all sorts of forms. It might be your suppliers, your board, your stockholders, or government agencies—and especially your clients and customers.

I know a home builder who regularly deals with two different city officials who are responsible for making sure builders are complying with city codes. He never knows which of the two will show up, but he knows which one he prefers. One of the city officials is of the reasonable variety. He points out problems and insists that they be addressed in a timely manner, but he is fair and empathetic to the realities the builder faces. The other is . . . well, a jerk. He seems consumed by the power of his position. One day he showed up at a job site after four straight days of rain and insisted that the construction crews immediately clean the mud off the street. Not at the end of the day or a couple of times during the day, but each time a clump of mud dropped onto the pavement.

The builder does what he loves in the service of people who love what he does, but that particular city official is just darn hard to love. He loves him anyway because that's the only way he can really serve the other people—the future homeowners, in particular—who actually share his love for building quality homes at reasonable prices. And he never loses hope that someday the jerk will become a fan and share in his love.

For most companies, the external stakeholders who we need to love us fall into the broad category of *the customers*. If we work for a consumer goods company, for instance, those customers could be the buyers at major retailers, but they are also the shoppers who pluck our products off the shelves and scan them through the self-checkout machines. The customers could be clients, shoppers, investors, or patrons at a sushi restaurant. It's the people we count on to give up something they have—mainly time and money—in exchange for something we provide so that we can keep doing what we love.

When they catch our shared-love vision and love it as much as we do, then they keep buying what we're selling, and they help us sell it to everyone they know.

10

PICTURES OF
RECIPROCITY

*You have not lived today until you have done something for
someone who can never repay you.*
—JOHN BUNYAN

THE ENERGY,
AUDACITY, AND PROOF

The entire premise of this book hinges on the final element of my LEAP model for Extreme Leadership. That element is proof. If there's no proof that love is just damn good business, then what's the point, right?

Remember near the beginning of this book when I talked about the three typical reactions I get from leaders when I bring up the idea of love as a business principle? Some leaders, whether they openly admit it or not, believe love has no place in business. None. Others see love as valuable in business because love, as a concept, is intrinsically important; therefore, the business must sacrifice at times to honor the high principle of love. And then there's the group that sees love as both intrinsically a good thing *and* actually good for business.

If there's no proof, then the first group is right, the second group is honorable albeit a bit naïve, and the third group, which includes me, of course, is both naïve and wrong.

So how do you prove that love is just damn good business? Well, it's not easy, but few things of great value are. Love isn't easy, so why should measuring its value be easy? But it is possible, and hopefully, you've already picked up on a few of the ways you can do it.

I've already mentioned that using a variation of the Net Promoter Score is a good way to measure the degree to which you are doing what you love in the service of people who love what you do. But it's also an obvious tool that helps measure how much others love what you do.

Elay Cohen, the SalesHood CEO I've mentioned a few times in this book, is an avid fan of the NPS. He doesn't check his sales pipeline multiple times a day, he told me, but he looks at his Net Promoter Score every chance he gets. He learns what he and his team are doing well and, more important, how they can improve.

"When we get a zero score from someone—because it happens, people give you zeros—they write something down," he told me. "No matter what they say, they get an e-mail from me and a handwritten thank-you note. 'Thank you for taking the time to tell us we can be better. We'd love a chance to learn from you.' People are floored. They think, 'Holy cow, you just did what? Who does that? Do people even read this stuff?'"

Cohen gets hundreds of pieces of NPS feedback a month, and he never sends handwritten thank-you notes to the customers who give him a 10—just the ones who fired a zero in his direction. If he can make those customers feel good—if he can regain their trust and love—then, as he said, "they become a friend and a customer for life."

SalesHood, of course, has plenty of raving fans, and the evidence isn't just found in its NPS feedback. It's also found in the powerful testimonials that, to me, are the most valuable proof we can get to show the power of love in business. He calls them "Hood Love" stories, and many can be found on the company's website and YouTube channel.

"Literally, it's our customers saying what they love about working with SalesHood," he said. "And you can't make this shit up. They love us. They believe we're here to make them successful. We celebrate them; we help make our customers' careers because they can scale."

Internally, surveys that measure employee engagement provide a great measure of how well your team loves what you do. But in 2018, Cohen went a step further by hiring a seasoned human resources executive, Anne-Marie Canter, to interview all of the employees individually and record their feedback on what they loved about working for the company and where they saw areas for improvement. There were 44 comments about what people loved, and 10 about opportunities for improvement.

"There's a lot of love in there," Cohen said. "There's a lot of love and gratitude."

I've been wrong on many things in the course of six-plus decades of life. But I *know* I'm not wrong about the power of love as a business principle. I hope you've seen plenty of proof along the way, but I want to offer up just a little bit more, especially as it relates to reciprocity on investment. That's the kicker in our credo statement. Do what you love in the service of people *who love what you do*. If people love what you do, then you've elevated your game to a place that's undeniably, unequivocally . . .

damn...

good...

business.

I know this because I've seen it in companies all over the world, including all of the examples I've referenced previously in this book. Here are four more—a startup founded out of love, an established company that used love to avoid complacency and grow stronger, an executive who has witnessed the power of kindness, and a company that emerged from bankruptcy and used love to energize its failing culture. All are now experiencing record growth by operationalizing love in the way they do business.

BRYON STEPHENS, PIVOTAL GROWTH PARTNERS

Bryon Stephens believes love is damn good business. Not just because it *sounds* like a great idea, but because putting it into practice for decades has produced undeniable results. It's the foundation, he will tell you, of the formula that took a working-class kid from Logansport, Indiana, with a high school education and a job washing dishes to top leadership positions in the restaurant industry, including president of one of America's fastest-growing pizza chains.

"Everybody likes to feel good about love," Bryon said during the 2018 Extreme Leadership Experience, a three-day event we put on in San Diego. "But as a CEO, as an executive in an organization, I can tell you that . . . here's the bottom line: If this can't deliver results, radical results, then it's just a fun idea. It's not going to be one where businesses step up and take it, because it has to deliver results. And this is proof—the career I've been lucky enough to have is proof that this delivers results."

Bryon worked with me as CEO of the Extreme Leadership Institute during our company's formation. He is now the cofounder of Pivotal Growth Partners, a consulting group that helps up-and-coming franchise brands scale. Before that, he spent 14 years helping grow Marco's Pizza from a regional chain in Ohio to more than 900 stores in 35 states and four countries. He rose to the position of president and chief development officer (you might remember him from an episode of the TV show *Undercover Boss*) before he retired from the company in 2017.

It's been an incredible journey for a guy whose mom worked three jobs when he was growing up and whose dad was raised as an orphan and never went to college. Bryon's parents, in fact, pushed him toward a job at a local factory rather than a university education, and before he turned 20, he had earned enough money to take out loans on a house, a truck, a camper trailer, and a boat. He was living the good life, at least that's what he thought. Then the factory workers went on strike, the paychecks stopped coming, and the bills continued to show up in his mailbox. That's when he took a job washing dishes at a Holiday Inn.

"I didn't get that job because I was saving up to go to college," he said. "This was my job. That was the job I got with the skills that I had and what was available."

When he bemoaned the turn of events in his career to his father, he got some profound advice: "It's not what a man does for a living that brings him honor. It's how he does what he does." His father suggested that Bryon "get out there and be the best dishwasher that they've ever seen and see where that takes you."

That's exactly what he did. Bryon came to that sink with a great attitude, worked hard each day, helped the cooks when they needed something, sang songs out loud, and occasionally danced while he did it, all with the hope of getting a promotion with slightly better pay. It wasn't long before the owner of the hotel took notice and offered him something even better: a management-track position with his company. It paid less than the factory job, he was told, but the long-term potential was much better.

Bryon's career took off as he realized that injecting love and enthusiasm into his work led to some amazing opportunities.

"The thing it did was put into me the love of four things," he said. "The love of restaurants, the love of franchising, the love of leadership, and the love of learning."

Restaurants? He loved cooking, serving the staff and the customers, the marketing, the training, the entertainment, and the energy created by his passion for it.

Franchising? He loved the opportunity it gave to local entrepreneurs with a dream, the ability to help those owners build a business and take pride in it, and the fact that it changed people's lives—just as it had changed his life.

Leadership? He loved being a trainer, coach, and teammate, the idea that he got to quarterback the team, the pressure of delivering results, and, yes, the accolades that came with success.

Learning? He made up for his lack of a formal education because he loved learning from every single person with whom he came in contact. He loved reading, preparing, and walking into the boardroom with the confidence that he was as well informed as anybody else in the room.

But here's the critical piece of his story: Bryon began to manifest all of that love in the way he managed and led others. In turn, that love caused his team to love what they were doing, and his businesses to prosper in ways that exceeded everyone's expectations, except Bryon's.

Early in his budding restaurant career, Bryon's first management position was at a Ponderosa Steakhouse. This wasn't just any Ponderosa Steakhouse—it was one of the *lowest-performing* Ponderosa Steakhouses in the entire chain. In fact, he took the job knowing the owners already were planning to close it.

In his first speech to his employees, Bryon told his new team their Ponderosa was ranked as one of the worst in the company.

"Every store in the country serves the same food," he told them, "has the same marketing, has the same carpeting, has the same roof. Everything about it is the same. There's one difference. You know what that is?"

No one knew.

"It's the people," he told them. "When they say this is the worst store in the country, they're saying you guys are the worst in the country, and I don't buy it. I think we can show them that we're the best in the country."

They set a goal of going from worst to first within two years.

Bryon gave the team a vision, and he made sure they knew he believed in them and their ability to take the store to No. 1. Then he backed up his words with actions. He worked tirelessly, seldom taking a day off. And when a district supervisor toured the restaurant and took off points because of the worn carpet that the corporate office wouldn't replace, Bryon took his entire $100 a month in discretionary manager's money and, without getting approval, spent it on a new carpet that he ordered from a local merchant.

Then he looked at all the rules he was supposed to follow and figured out how to make them work for a store operating in a low-income, inner-city environment. For instance, many restaurants have a rule that if you don't show up on time, you're fired. Makes sense, right?

But instead of jumping straight to punitive measures to discourage tardiness, Bryon asked a very simple, often-overlooked question: "Why weren't people getting to work on time?"

The answer, in retrospect, seems obvious. And it had nothing to do with people's attitudes.

Most of his employees, as it turned out, didn't have cars. They either walked to work or rode the bus, and public transportation in Gary, Indiana, was notoriously inconsistent.

"If I wanted people there on time," he said, "I needed to set up a system to allow them to be there on time." That meant Bryon sometimes would get in his car, drive to employees' homes, pick them up, and bring them to work.

Now ask yourself this question: "If my restaurant employees were consistently showing up for work in dirty uniforms, as many of Bryon's were, what would I do about it?"

Again, Bryon asked why. And, again, the answer was simple.

Many of his employees didn't have washers and dryers at home. So Bryon collected their uniforms and washed them himself.

Then he set up a "safe zone" in the store where employees who were in school could do their homework, which he and others helped them with. He went to their weddings. He went to the funerals of their friends and family members. He even loaned them money from his own pocket to help them do things they otherwise couldn't afford.

"What we did was demonstrate love for them," he said.

Rather than leading with the carrot (rewards) or the stick (fear) or by lighting a fire under his employees, Bryon stoked the fire burning inside his employees' hearts by believing in them and caring for them in deeply meaningful and tangible ways.

One year later, Ponderosa Steakhouse 319 in Gary, Indiana, was voted the best steakhouse in the Ponderosa system, and Bryon was promoted to area supervisor, the fastest ascension to that position in the history of that company.

"We made sure they knew we weren't posers," he said. "We loved them, and what we got back was tenfold. The happiest moment of my life was not winning the award. Three of the young people who didn't know where their lives were going—they were just people like me, a dishwasher at a Ponderosa—became managers within the Ponderosa system the year after we won that award. That's what caring about people can do."

SHAWN MAHONEY, OAC SERVICES

What's the most dangerous threat to a thriving business? That's a tough question, and, frankly, there might not be a definitive answer. But I can tell you that complacency is right up there near the top, not just because of the damage it causes but because it's so hard to spot until long after the damage is done.

Shawn Mahoney, managing principal of Seattle-based construction management, architecture, and engineering firm OAC, recognized that he worked for a great company with great people and a great history, but he was determined to build on that success and not take it for granted. He became passionate about helping OAC create a more formalized understanding of its values and its culture so the company could more intentionally avoid potential pitfalls while growing as an organization.

"My frustration as an emerging leader was that it was one thing to say internally that we had a great culture, but if we weren't showing it, we had a problem," he told me. "To grow our enterprise, we needed to identify our foundation and our soul."

OAC, a privately held firm founded in 1955 that provides architecture, engineering, and construction management services, has weathered all sorts of storms, and it has evolved to meet the changing demands of the marketplace. Until a few years ago, however, it had no framework for aligning its mission, vision, and core values around the strengths of its culture. Mahoney used my LEAP model for that framework, but it wasn't something the company adopted overnight. In fact, it took several years.

Mahoney heard me speak in 2013 at the Construction Management Association's annual convention, and he intuitively knew that love, energy, audacity, and proof would have an important role in OAC's future. The company already operated on those values, but he couldn't just return to Seattle and send out a memo announcing that OAC was becoming a LEAP organization. First, he needed the company's other six principals to unanimously embrace the idea, and some of them had an "if it ain't broke, don't fix it" mindset. Second, he needed to sell it to the 70-plus employees, most of whom had an understandably low tolerance for flavor-of-the-month management best practices.

Since the company was doing well and had a healthy culture, Mahoney took a slower approach to formalizing love as a key component of their business. First, he and five other OAC leaders attended the Extreme Leadership Summit in 2014. Then he and a few others participated in an Extreme Leadership Certification Program. By January 2015, when Mahoney was named the firm's managing principal, he felt there was enough momentum to test the message more widely throughout the organization. They organized a series of events that May—LEAP Week, they called it—to share the big ideas around love, energy, audacity, and proof, and then they began exploring ways to adopt them as a framework at OAC.

The measured rollout of the program allowed for an organic experience. They began by announcing that management was committing to a more inclusive, open-door leadership approach. They told employees this would begin with a survey to learn what employees valued. They would then form four employee-led committees that would help determine the direction of a new framework.

"We are no longer just going to make all the decisions at the top and push it down," they said. "We aren't going to be in a secluded room where you have to make an appointment to make an appointment to see us. We are going to get your feedback and love and care enough about you to value what you think."

OAC had used committees in the past, often without the best of results. That's because the committees were run by a member of the leadership team.

"It was like saying, 'I'm empowering you to do everything, but check with me first,'" said Mahoney.

This time, they took a different approach. The new committees—culture, communications, talent, and growth—were led by employees, who established key objectives and results that were measured against cultivating love, generating energy, inspiring audacity, and providing proof. They made recommendations for everything from community service projects to policies that would shape the way OAC operated. And they regularly reported on the plans and progress of their work.

For the first time, the employees felt like they were making the decisions. They not only bought into LEAP as a framework but they also adopted a modified version of the credo you've been reading about in this book as their vision statement: "We do what we love in the service of people who love what we do." And their core values? Cultivate love, generate energy, inspire audacity, and provide proof. Eventually they crafted a mission statement that spoke to their values and was supported by the framework: "Serve our clients and communities as trusted partners to design, build, and improve where people live, work, learn, and play."

It took nine months to come up with the mission, vision, and values, but Mahoney said it was worth the wait.

"Every single person felt part of it, and they all were embracing it," he said. "If we had just rolled it out at LEAP Week, there wouldn't have been any steam. Now there's ownership in it."

Because of that ownership, LEAP is incorporated into nearly every aspect of the business—including performance reviews, the hiring process, internships, and community service.

Mahoney originally felt an immediate connection to the LEAP model in part because he could see those components in the people who worked at OAC. It wasn't something he had to create so much as bring out of the shadows and into the light.

"The love and the energy were a slam dunk," he said. "And in our business, as in any consulting business, providing proof is the deliverable you have to have."

Formalizing it and embracing LEAP has helped them bring those values to life in more notable and measurable ways. As a professional services firm, for instance, OAC always has recruited and valued people who value relationships. But like many organizations, they never used the word *love* to describe how they operated as a business.

"It took some time for people to recognize that love is an essential part of how they do business and then just to get used to saying the word," Mahoney said. "I think the first couple times, it feels a little funny, right? Especially for engineers, architects, contractors. But they are the first ones to give their colleague a hug after accomplishing a major task. So once you take a little while to socialize it, they get it."

OAC had workshops with exercises that helped employees personalize the values so they could see, for instance, what love meant to them when it came to clients, vendors, partners, and, most important, each other. They realized, for instance, that love encompassed values like trust, respect, listening, and caring—all things they already believed in.

Putting terminology and language around their values helped OAC incorporate them into their formal awards and recognition programs, and it also helped them become more intentional about sharing their values outwardly. They started by putting the mission, vision, and values on the internal website, then on the public website, and more recently, in their proposals to clients and on social media sites.

"It's definitely making a difference," Mahoney said. "There's a firm in Seattle, Big Fish Games, for example, that's really committed to their mission, vision, and core values, so they are looking for other companies with similar values and the same discipline. Facebook [which is another OAC client] is a great example of where it really resonates with them."

The feedback, internally and externally, is providing proof that LEAP is working for OAC. The survey conducted in 2017 showed marked improvement from the initial baseline survey in 2015. OAC asked employees for feedback on a number of statements grouped into 12 categories, and only those who strongly agreed, agreed, or somewhat agreed were considered favorable responses when tabulating the results. In every category, the percentage of favorable responses increased from the baseline survey. By industry standards, a 5 percent increase is considered difficult to achieve and therefore quite significant. Yet 9 out of 12 of the categories had an increase of at least 5 percent. Culture (plus 11.60 percent) and workplace environment (plus 14.22 percent) showed the biggest increases, and the average increase was 6.75 percent.

In 2016, *Seattle Business* released its list of best companies to work for in the state of Washington, and OAC ranked No. 14 among midsized companies. By 2017, OAC had shot up to No. 2. Those rankings are more than nice ego biscuits. They also have led to new relationships with other leaders of companies on that list, which has expanded OAC's business opportunities. And, of course, they've provided proof that what they are doing is working.

Jenna Lynch, president and chief client officer of the Extreme Leadership Institute, who worked as a consultant for OAC, said OAC provides a prime example of how a great company can proactively identify and build on its strengths.

"I work with a lot of companies, and OAC was not a toxic company when I came in," Lynch said. "I don't want people to think that they only need LEAP if they are in a dismal state of business and about to close the doors. That's not the case at all. It's really important to know that companies can come in that are already great but that could be exponentially better. Shawn was an emerging leader who wanted to get in front of this, and he built a structure that made OAC even stronger and better."

OAC is experiencing unprecedented, explosive growth. When Mahoney and I first met in 2014, OAC was a company with 50 people in three offices that did $9.8 million in annual revenue. By the end of 2018, they employed 148 people in seven offices and had $28.5 million in revenue.

"Since Leap Week," Mahoney told me, "we have grown 142 percent, and revenues have increased 150 percent. We are a $40 million company now annualized."

JILL LUBLIN,
AUTHOR AND PR EXPERT

Jill Lublin arrived in Las Vegas for a speaking engagement only to discover that the hotel where she had booked a room didn't have her reservation, nor did it have an available room. It was late and she was tired, but things got worse before they got better. She called 18 hotels before she found a room at the Marriott Renaissance, and it was 2 a.m. by the time she walked through the front doors and up to the check-in counter.

The clerk at the desk had talked to her on the phone and already had given her a discounted rate, but she took one look at Jill's face and made an executive decision.

"You know what, forget $169," she said as she checked Jill in. "Let's make it $129. I can tell you've had a tough night."

For the rest of her stay—which turned into three nights because she never went back to her original hotel—Jill was treated with respect and kindness. It earned the hotel two more nights worth of business, but it also gave Jill an example of kindness that she shares when she speaks to groups or to friends such as me.

That clerk's act of love provided real business value for her employer because it created a customer who loved what she did and loved the fact that the hotel had empowered her to do it.

"They've got policies and procedures that they have to follow," Jill told me, "but they're smart enough to give their people some decision-making abilities and possibilities."

Earlier I shared a formula: kindness + high standards = love at work. Obviously, I see kindness as a critical component to love in the context of business. Jill feels so strongly about kindness as a business principle that she wrote a book about it, *The Profit of Kindness*. And she teaches that there are seven key elements of kindness that create a positive return: treating employees, customers, clients, and anyone else connected to your business with respect, compassion, generosity, positivity, gratitude, flexibility, and patience.

Those acts of kindness, which I see as acts of love, will be returned in kind, so to speak. In practical terms, customers are more likely to recommend you, employees will complain less and work more, and everyone will simply be more forgiving during those inevitable times when you, because you are human, fail.

"When something bad does happen," Jill told me, "there is an opportunity to say, 'It's OK. I know this doesn't happen a lot.'"

In her book, Jill cites examples from Honda, KIND bars, Airbnb, CEO Space, Coca-Cola, Zappos, LL Bean, and Kleenex, among others, as companies that have operated with enough consistent kindness to earn positive returns for their businesses.

"Kindness is a currency," she said. "Imagine that your clients are referral partners, which, of course, is a kind thing that brings you actual currency—it brings you actual business. That is the ultimate kindness: referring someone. That's a currency and it results in true business."

When you invest in love as a business principle and in the kindness that comes with it, you reap the rewards—referrals, loyalty, employee engagement, retention, forgiveness, and on and on the list goes.

"It's the actual piece that will make a company stand out and be remembered, even more than annual reports and bottom-line P&Ls," she said.

MITCH LUCIANO,
TRAILER BRIDGE

Trailer Bridge is one of those companies that has plenty of reason to toot its own horn. The Jacksonville, Florida, *Business Journal* uses anonymous feedback from area employees to create its annual list of "Best Places to Work," and Trailer Bridge has been in the top 10 in its category every year since 2016. In 2018, it won the Silver Bell Humanitarian Award for its contributions to relief efforts in Puerto Rico following Hurricane Maria. And on top of all that, the company is more profitable than it's ever been in its 25-plus-year history.

Not bad for a company that emerged from bankruptcy in 2012, went through four CEOs during the ensuing three years, and was only earning about a 1 percent return per year when Mitch Luciano took over in 2014. Luciano was given three directives: One, fix the financial bottom line by increasing profitability. Two, fix the culture. And three, don't let No. 2 get in the way of No. 1.

Luciano, who had been with the shipping and logistics company since 2012, knew the strengths and weaknesses of the culture, and he immediately began implementing a love-focused leadership approach that turned the leaky ship into a powerful force in its community and industry.

Previous efforts to revive the company had focused largely on processes—everything from expense reports to the equipment maintenance program. Those were important, but Luciano wanted to address the core problem, not just the surface-level symptoms. He wanted answers to deeper, more difficult questions, like these: "Why do people hate it here?" "Why do we have such huge turnover?" "Why is it like pulling teeth to get information out of people?"

"They didn't look into those things," he told me, "but I knew that's what had to be done."

The drastic changes that were needed wouldn't be easy to implement. Trailer Bridge employed about 110 men and women who ranged in age from 22 to 73 and who had very different cultural and economic backgrounds. Gaining alignment among such a diverse group was a challenge in itself. Plus, the company's employees—including the top-ranking executives on Luciano's team—had very little appetite for another change in leadership philosophy. They had grown accustomed to working in silos within a culture that focused on operational execution at the expense of relationships between coworkers or with customers.

Luciano understood that the power of love is found in the trust it creates over time, so he made slow, modest changes while focusing on the consistency of his leadership behaviors. Some of the initial changes were cosmetic, but meaningful. He wouldn't accept the CEO title, for instance, until he had earned more trust as the company's leader. He also lowered the walls of the cubicles so people could see each other and interact more naturally. He put in some new furniture and new carpeting. And he bought Ping-Pong and foosball tables. But he didn't stop with surface-level changes. To put it in shipping terms, he knew he needed more than a shiny deck. He needed to repair the hull as well. So he created a leadership team that embraced and modeled his approach for building a culture that valued loving one another.

"I don't think we ever said we would change the culture," Luciano said. "We talked about improving the environment and their experience. The objective was to make it a great experience for people."

Soon, the culture began to change, and Trailer Bridge formalized Luciano's leadership approach. Indie Bollman, who took over as head of HR in July 2015, worked with Luciano on a training program with the objective of creating a common leadership philosophy and building team unity. The first phase laid a foundation and included assessments that allowed each leader to receive anonymous feedback from others.

"It was difficult," Luciano said. "I got mine from 15 or 16 people, and it took me a while to swallow that pill."

One of the more challenging parts of the first phase came when Bollman and Luciano introduced the "love" component to a leadership team that included veterans of the Marines and the Navy. Luciano saw a look in their eyes that told him they weren't much interested in what they assumed would be a touchy-feely approach to leadership. The love component, he explained, might include a hug here or there if that fits your style and that's what someone needs, but it's really more about consistently respecting others and taking care of their needs.

"Kindness, to me, is love," he said. "I really focused in on the emotional side of love and things like respect, kindness, and loyalty. Those are all things that create love."

He also gave them tangible examples of what love looks like in leadership.

"Love is when people walk into your office and say, 'Do you have 5 minutes?' and you know it's not going to be 5 minutes—it's going to be 30," he said. "You know it as soon as they walk in, and you turn your computer off, and you look them in the eye, and you pay attention to everything they have to say, and you actually hear them."

The second phase of the Trailer Bridge leadership program promoted the idea of mentorship and helping others become their best. This was particularly important, Luciano said, because Trailer Bridge had developed a culture of information hoarding.

Some leaders hoarded information because they feared releasing it might contribute to their obsolescence. Others simply didn't trust anyone else to use the information correctly.

"We had to make them think about the people on their team they could teach and really share information with," Luciano said.

Then he promised them he wasn't asking them to share that information so he could dump someone with a $100,000 salary and replace her with someone making $60,000.

"That's not my goal," he told them. "Again, a moment of trust."

Most of the leaders who went through the program bought into the idea, but at least one resisted to the point where he was let go.

"If you're a hoarder of information, you're no longer valuable to me," Luciano said. "If you feed and educate those around you, then you're more valuable. Those who were hoarders, they're no longer a part of Trailer Bridge."

Tough love, in other words.

The third part of the training focused on customer relationships—using love as a foundational mindset for providing customer care.

The results of the changes at Trailer Bridge have been dramatically positive for the employees, for the customers, and for the bottom line.

The employees have gotten more from the cultural transformation than a chance to play Ping-Pong on their breaks. They helped define the culture they wanted, the type of leadership they needed, and the company's formal values—what they call "the Trailer Bridge 12," or the "TB12." Their feedback surveys and reviews no longer recommend the traditional "start, stop, continue." Now they focus on "love it, learn it, fix it" to plan their next steps.

Turnover at Trailer Bridge has decreased, more employees are recommending the company to their friends, and independent surveys are giving the company high marks on employee satisfaction. Luciano especially appreciates the firsthand accounts of how things have changed. Employees have told him they had been "hanging on for the paycheck" for 10 years, but now they loved their jobs and their coworkers, and their lives were better.

"Our employees are bringing us quality candidates," Bollman said. "If that's not enough, the people who apply on our website are quality talent. I didn't see that coming, but it's changed that whole process."

Customers, meanwhile, also are seeing Trailer Bridge in a new light. Surveys in 2015 painted a picture of the company as a bargain carrier that won business by competing primarily on price. Now Trailer Bridge is still seen as competitive on price but its advantage for customers is in its commitment to service.

Two years ago, for example, the company sailed to the Caribbean twice a week, but often they would simply cancel a trip if the ship wasn't at least 70 percent full. Why? Because, according to the balance sheet, the expense didn't justify the revenue the freight was producing.

As a customer, can you imagine booking a shipment to Puerto Rico and being told at the last minute that the boat was canceled because it wasn't full enough? That would happen frequently. As a result, customers lost faith that their cargo would arrive on schedule, and the service reviews were dismal, to say the least.

If the company really loved its customers, they would sail anyway—no matter how empty the ship, or how much of a loss they would take on that particular run. So the Trailer Bridge team decided to "always sail," regardless of capacity, because that is how you keep your word to the customer.

The employees of Trailer Bridge also are much more solutions focused. They might not be able to do exactly what a customer wants, but now they look for alternative ideas that will address the root problem, sometimes even when there's no direct financial incentive for the company. Because that's what you do when you love somebody.

One customer, for instance, arrived to pick up a dump truck that he bought and had shipped to Jacksonville from San Juan. When he tried to drive it away, he discovered that the truck was dead. Three Trailer Bridge employees helped him get it started, but the truck broke down on a nearby highway. So the Trailer Bridge mechanics went out and got it running. The customer sent Luciano a two-page thank-you note.

"Your angels saved my day," he wrote. "I didn't know what I was going to do. I was going to be stuck sleeping in a dump truck on the side of the highway. Instead, I called them, and they were there to help me. They had no reason to help me. They didn't gain anything out of it. I just want you to know what amazing people you have working at Trailer Bridge."

The letter brought tears of joy to Luciano's eyes.

"They went out and did their own thing," he said. "That's why I take pride in my team. They do these things on their own. A perfect stranger to them, but they did it, and that's what matters."

As customers realized they could trust Trailer Bridge with their shipments, business increased and the number of times they sailed at less than 70 percent capacity dropped dramatically. In 2015, they typically sailed at 75 to 80 percent full. Now their average ship sails at 95 to 100 percent capacity.

"That had a huge impact on our results," Luciano said. "That obviously had direct results on our bottom line."

They also have seen an increase in customer retention.

In 2015, Luciano's first full year as president of the company, the number of returning customers went up to 20 percent, a number they've matched or bettered each year since. The company has seen record profitability each year for four consecutive years, with earnings from 2015 through 2017 greater than the previous 23 years *combined*. 2018 yielded the greatest revenues and earnings in the history of the company, and they're opening new offices around the United States. The board and the owners of the enterprise are, as you can imagine, quite pleased, to say the least.

Still, Luciano sees Trailer Bridge as a work in progress.

"It takes years to build a culture, and you can tear it down in a day," he said. "You have to keep doing it. You have to keep focusing on it."

11

REAPING WHAT
YOU'VE SOWN

*If your company is having trouble attracting fabulous people,
it is because your company sucks.*
—Tom Peters

NOW WHAT?

This chapter is a bit tricky.

As you've noticed, each section in this book ends with a chapter that's very how-to focused, a chapter that loads you up with practical tips for living out what was described in the previous chapters. This section is all about the third part of our key phrase—do what you love in the service of people *who love what you do*. This chapter is supposed to provide practical how-tos for getting people to love what you do. But is that even possible?

We all want to be loved. It's a basic need, right? The thing is, we can't *make* anyone love us—or what we do. Reciprocal love is a choice, and, frankly, we shouldn't want it any other way. We want people to *freely* love what we do. At the same time, that doesn't mean that we can't proactively work to create this type of reciprocal love for the work that we do.

I'm not much of a gardener, but I know enough to use it for an analogy. Gardeners plant the right seeds in the right places, provide water and some fertilizer. They nurture the seedlings that sprout. They get rid of the weeds. And if they do all the right things, then they've created an environment where something good can grow and thrive. They can't make it grow, but they can give it the best possible circumstances for growth.

The same is true with love. We can't make others love us or the work we do. But we can plant the right seeds and give them the best possible circumstances for love to blossom. That's what the tips you'll find in this chapter will help you do.

DESCRIBE YOUR DISTINCTIVE CHARACTERISTIC

Let's start with a fundamental question: why should anyone love what you do?

That's not a rhetorical question. I'm really asking. Spend some time thinking about it. Reflect on it. Watch the people around you, and see what they embody that helps describe it. Ask them and yourself these questions: "What do we as a company really do and do better than anyone else on the planet? And how can each of us—as Extreme Leaders—embody that in the way that we approach our work each day?"

One of your jobs as an Extreme Leader is to cut quickly through the transactional elements of the work, get to the essence of its meaning, and then lay it out clearly for everyone involved. This can involve the great, big vision for the organization or the vision for a particular project that you're about to lead. Either way, carve out some solo time to reflect on and answer the following questions. Write down your responses and answers:

- What is this company or project really about, beyond its obvious transactional activities and details?

- What kind of impact are we trying to have on the lives of our customers and end users?

- How does each of us contribute to the enhancement of our end user's life and business?

- What magnificent future will I and my colleagues create together?

- What future reality will make my current OS!Ms worthwhile?

- Am I in love with the picture of the future that we all are trying to bring to pass?

Feel free to add similar questions and allow yourself to follow your musings wherever they take you.

When you're satisfied with your answers (you'll know because of how energized and inspired you'll feel), the next step is really quite simple: Talk about it with your team. Share it and ask people to respond. Ask them to think about the same questions and share their answers at a subsequent meeting. Then watch what happens to the energy of the team.

IMPROVE YOUR NIGHT VISION

If we want people to love what we do, we need to create a vision for the future that they will love. To do that, we have to create a shared love of a future state that's different from our present. At the same time, that future state has to be realistic. It needs to stretch us, but it can't be unattainable.

Futurists analyze what's going on today and then look over the horizon of time to tell us what's likely to happen in the future. An applied futurist also looks at the trends, records, and observations and then makes some predictions about what might happen. But the applied futurist goes beyond anticipating the future state and begins acting in ways that create it.

People might love your grand vision for something, but they won't really get behind it in a consistent, powerful way until they see you acting on it in consistently powerful ways.

Being an applied futurist is a direct application of the leadership practice of vision. It is getting a picture of the future and then offering products or services today and taking actions today that will make that future a reality. In *Leading the Revolution*, Gary Hamel points out that the goal of the visionary leader isn't to "speculate on what might happen, but to imagine what you can actually make happen. Companies fail to create the future not because they failed to predict it, but because they fail to imagine it." So if you want to create a shared-love vision, then become a futurist and apply that to the products, services, and approaches that you take with your teams and your customers.

We are fortunate to live in a world where applied futurists have bombarded us with things we never knew we needed— watches that count how many steps we take each day, phones that take pictures and videos, running shoes that have air in them, and TV shows that stream on our television sets.

We didn't need these or want these until somebody created them. Now we find it hard to live without them.

Here are some simple ideas for becoming an applied futurist.

Pay Attention

Here's another quote from Gary Hamel's *Leading the Revolution*: "Every day, companies get blindsided by the future. . . . Yet the future never arrives as a surprise to *everyone* in an organization. Someone, somewhere, was paying attention. For these heretics and novelty addicts, tomorrow's opportunities are every bit as real and inevitable as today's sunrise." Become one of those people in the organization who is paying attention—who looks at the future as being as inevitable as today's sunrise.

If you pay attention, of course, you'll notice things worth remembering. Write them down. Don't get caught up in what they mean. Just record your observations. If you ever find yourself thinking, "Oh, that's interesting, I'll remember that, I need to come back and think about that later," I guarantee that you will not remember it. Write it down.

Look Everywhere

You don't need to travel all that far in search of ideas. Visit a bookstore (brick and mortar, if you can still find one) or some other place that has a large periodical section. Then scan the titles of the magazines, and pick up one that you have absolutely no interest in.

The first thing you will notice is the incredible number of sub-cultures and interests in this country that have nothing to do with your life. This is a wonderful way to be exposed to them. You don't have to be a wrangler in Montana to understand cowboys. Just pick up *Cowboy Weekly*, and take a look at what cowboys are buying. Pick up a copy of *Tattoo World* or *Body Piercing International*. Look through them, and jot down your observations. Again, don't get caught up in what this all means; just make the observations. Also, pay attention to the emerging trends on television. Go to the mall, a park, or a big-box store. Think about what you see, write some notes, and start asking the right questions: "What did I find that was interesting? What does that tell me about our culture? What can I learn from that?"

Talk About It

After you have made your observations and you have encouraged the people you work with to make similar explorations, carve out a meeting every so often—once a month or a couple times a quarter—and compare notes on what's going on in the world. Then start asking about the possible impact these might have on your business.

Are there things you are seeing that you can begin to incorporate, use, and develop in your products and offerings that can serve your clients in ways they don't even know they need? How might you apply what you're learning in ways that create love-centric ROI?

GO BACK TO THE FUTURE

If you're still struggling to cast a vision that people will love, then perhaps you need to strap on your Marty McFly shoes and take a trip to the future. Envision what you're striving to create, and then describe that end state in vivid detail. Here's a simple process that you can do on your own or with your team.

Roll the clock forward, and imagine that your company is experiencing phenomenal, earth-shattering success. Then "remember" how it all happened by doing the following:

- Making a list of everything you accomplished as a team

- Writing down all the ways you and each of your team members gained personally from having worked together

- Describing the legacy you've left, the reputation you've established individually and collectively, and how your clients describe the impact you've had on them

Now, using those notes as a guide, come back to the present day and write at least one paragraph to complete this statement: "Here's what our success will look like . . ."

DO SOME SPRING CLEANING

You don't have to wait until spring to do this. In fact, don't wait. Start today with a good, old-fashioned eradication of anything that doesn't help you create the right culture for others to love what you do. There's no time like the present to purge the energy suckers around you:

- Get rid of the unnecessary bureaucratic policies and procedures in your work life that sap you and your folks of the energy required to achieve greatness.

- Encourage yourself and others to root out and discard any work that hinders your cause.

- Determine what you might be doing that keeps you from fulfilling your goals and dreams. Now, stop doing them. That's easier said than done, I know, and you might have some false stops along the way. When that happens, recommit to your commitment.

- Figure out what must be changed to make your office a more interesting, exciting, and awesome place to work.

BRIDGE THE GAPS

Let's end this discussion with some advice based on the real-world example I shared in Chapter 10 involving Trailer Bridge. As you'll recall, Mitch Luciano took over a company that was struggling financially and that needed a cultural makeover. People weren't doing what they loved, they weren't serving others very well, and their work wasn't loved by others.

Luciano knew he had to rebuild trust to create a new energy at Trailer Bridge. Here are few ways he incorporated love into his business practices that you can too.

Care for People

Love begins with caring for people and for your work. Luciano set that as an expectation from other leaders because that's what he wanted from everyone in the company.

"They weren't cared for; therefore, they didn't care about what they were doing, which was passed on to customers and vendors, and ultimately was passed on to our reputation and led to bank-ruptcy," he said. "It's a direct correlation."

Caring for others began with getting to know them—by name.

"We had name tags everywhere," Luciano said. "I took them all down. I said, 'We shouldn't need name tags for 110 employees. We should know each other.'"

Luciano learned everyone's name, said hello to people each day, asked questions, listened, learned personal stories, and dem-onstrated that he cared. Then he asked the other top leaders to do the same—to get out of their offices and cubicles, interact with people, and show some kindness. Luciano also began writing a personalized card to every employee on their birthday, collect-ing drawings of Trailer Bridge trucks made by employees' kids, holding regular town hall meetings, and having an open-door policy that allowed anyone to talk to him about whatever was on their mind.

"This doesn't take four hours a day," he has pointed out. "It may take 30 to 60 minutes a day. There's not a line outside your door. You can still get stuff done. And if you're a leader, you're ex-pected to be able to regroup and focus on what you're doing. If you can't, then there's something else you need to work on."

Hire Kind People, and Ditch Mean People

Luciano didn't arrive with an axe, but he didn't tolerate the cul-tural vipers who sucked the energy out of the organization. Within the first few months, for instance, he had easily identi-fied the person who, as he put it, was the "biggest nuisance" in the whole company.

"We got rid of that person," Luciano said. "And I immediately built some credibility."

Luciano invested time with problem employees, and some of them began to change their attitudes. Others left on their own. And a few were fired.

In addition to building trust and earning converts on the existing team, he also hired people who had positive energy. One of them was Indie Bollman, who became the fourth HR director the company had hired in three years. She spent her first few weeks just meeting people, asking questions, and doing a lot of listening.

"There clearly had been a lack of communication," she said. "My position did not have trust. I just had to put that out there as best I could."

Commit to the Commitment

Some leaders have no trouble saying no—even when they are saying yes. Luciano wanted to create a culture where everyone's yes meant something, a culture, in other words, where people did what they said they would do. Again, he had to model the big idea.

"The hardest part for me in those first few months was just committing to everything I said," Luciano remembered. "If I said we were going to do it, I had to do it, come hell or high water. That was the absolute No. 1 thing I had to do: keep my word."

In the old culture, employees might have made suggestions, and the leadership team might have agreed to implement them, but the ball often seemed to get dropped along the way. Then the blame game began: "I gave that responsibility to so-and-so and they never did it. It's their fault."

Luciano recalled a time when the company agreed to put in a new ice machine, but he realized a few weeks later that it had not been done.

"I [personally] ordered the ice machine," he said. "I committed to it, so I had to do it."

One key, he said, is not to make commitments you can't keep, which means leaders have to know when to say no.

"Somebody suggested 'beer pong Fridays,'" he recalled, "and I said, 'Guys, I would love to do that, but that's a no. That's something we can't do.' You tell them why, and they're OK with it."

Value the Value

The emphasis on building trusting relationships never came with a hall pass for people who weren't doing their jobs well or who weren't willing to do their part. There were no public floggings, but there was a high degree of accountability and a keen awareness of the business side of the business.

"We do this to make money," he said. "We're not a charity. Even if we were a charity, we would want to raise more money, so we could give away more money."

Everyone from the investors who own the company to the lowest-paid employee wants and needs to make money, and he has made sure every employee understands why that's so important.

"You guys don't come in here and work for free," he has told the Trailer Bridge family. "You guys want to pay bills. You want to drive a newer car. You want to have a nicer house, nicer clothes. You want to be able to pay for your kid's education. That's why we do all of this, so we can make more money as a company and, in turn, help you live a life where you can have everything you need and hopefully get most of the stuff you want."

PRAY FOR CROP FAILURE?

There's an old adage when it comes to the principle of sowing and reaping, and it goes like this: "If we truly reap what we sow, most of us should pray for crop failure."

That's certainly true for many leaders. If you are one of them, you can try that strategy. You can sow seeds of selfishness, greed, and dissent, then hope and pray that by some miracle you don't get what you actually deserve. Or you can sow seeds of love in your business. You can nurture those seeds by doing what you love in the service of the people around you. And you can reap the abundant rewards when those people demonstrate that they love what you do. The fruit you produce will be damn good business.

THE LOVE METRIC, PART III

. . . .

It's time for the final part of our love metric. After Part I, you re-flected on the idea of doing what you love. After Part II, you reflected on how well you are serving others.

Now, it's time to think about all of the parts of your life one more time.

> To what degree do others love the service you provide them?

Rate yourself on a scale of 1 to 10, and then answer these questions:

> Why did I give myself that score?

> What score would people who know me give me if I asked them to rate me on that same question (to what degree do they think others love the service I provide them)?

> What are three tangible things I can do in the next 30 days that would help me increase that score?

CONCLUSION:
GETTING DOWN TO BUSINESS

L ike all good business consultants, Ivan Misner cultivated referrals to generate new business, and that led him to a great idea.
He organized a small group of professionals he trusted and who
trusted him—everyone in the group loved each other and loved
what everyone else did—and they started meeting regularly at a
small coffee shop in Arcadia, California, and they began to proactively refer work to each other.

Ivan and his cohorts had decided up front that their group
would have only one person from any particular profession,
which meant they couldn't have two bankers or two attorneys or
two business consultants.

This wouldn't have worked too well for Noah when he was
populating the ark, but it was a great model for their budding referral group. It wasn't mercenary, like so many other networking
groups Ivan had experienced, nor was it only about socializing
with friends and having a good time. And because it was such a
great idea and it worked so well, other professionals wanted to
join. Since they wouldn't take new members from existing professions, Ivan began getting requests for him to help replicate the
model—to start new groups rather than expand his own.

"What I found was that people desperately needed what we
were doing, referrals, and they loved the format," Ivan told me.
"They loved the structure."

They loved it so much, in fact, that within 12 months of starting that first group in 1985, 20 more had formed. The next thing

Ivan knew, he no longer was a business consultant. He was the leader of a referral network that's now known as BNI (Business Network International). It has grown into a global network with more than 250,000 members and more than 8,900 chapters in over 75 countries around the world. As a business, BNI has grown every year for 34 consecutive years. Thirty-four straight years of growth. The technical term for that is "not too shabby."

I mentioned BNI briefly back in the beginning of this book because I was fortunate enough to deliver the opening keynote to their 2018 global conference in Bangkok. I thought it fitting to end the book by looking at BNI again because it so clearly represents how love can be damn good business anywhere in the world, regardless of industry or profession.

Love is the core business strategy that led to BNI's growth. And love is the business strategy that makes its chapters successful.

I didn't have to travel halfway around the world to know this, but let me tell you when the reality of it really hit me in a fresh and powerful way. When Ivan was introducing me as the speaker, he posed a question to the audience.

"In two words," he said, "what is the philosophy of BNI?"

There were around 3,000 people from 75 countries staring back at him. And immediately, almost with one voice, they responded with the same answer: "Givers Gain!"

I promise you won't find many organizations or companies in the world that have that type of unified understanding of what they are all about. It was incredible.

Givers Gain is the underlying philosophy of BNI and one of its seven core values. It means that by giving business to others, you will get business in return.

"This is how I created love in BNI—it was through my core values," Ivan told me. "People can really embrace the core values, and they really understand the culture. When they really understand the culture, they love the program, and they bleed burgundy [the company color]. Core values were the key for me to get people to love the program."

The other values—which all feed off of Givers Gain—are promoting lifelong learning, embracing the balance of traditions and innovation, having a positive attitude, building relationships, embracing accountability, and recognizing those who are contributing. Nothing in those values overtly says, "Get business," but the proof isn't hard to find. When Ivan and I spoke in late 2018, he told me BNI referrals had generated $14.2 billion for members over the trailing 12-month period.

"That's twice the gross domestic product of Liechtenstein," he told me.

"Maybe Liechtenstein needs a couple more chapters," I suggested.

"Well, it's a small country," he said, "but still, isn't that amazing that we generate twice the GDP of a small country?"

I had to agree. It's damn good business.

The point is that focusing on the elements that people can fall in love with results in numbers that prove profitability.

For this to work, of course, you have to actually live out the values that create a strong culture. If you do, you build trust, which gives people the freedom and the desire to speak the truth in love, which holds you accountable and promotes personal growth. And when you have that trust, you go to bat for each other, you recommend each other, and you forgive each other.

That's love. And it's just damn good business.

I've spoken all over the world, and regardless of the stop—whether it was in Asia, Europe, the Middle East, South America, or in my homeland of the United States—that message always has been well received. But the BNI audience was different because it was such an incredible mix of cultures, religions, traditions, industries, and professions, yet everyone was united around a core value. And when I dug deeper, I realized it wasn't just because there was an intellectual understanding of Givers Gain—it was because they love it.

I think they love it because they intuitively know it echoes the idea that love works—not just in theory, not just in theology, not just in personal relationships, not just in not-for-profits, but in all of life, and that includes business.

That gives me hope for what we can accomplish together as human beings.

I assume that you believe you've just read a business book. And you'd be right, of course. But that was really just my clever ploy to draw you in to the bigger story.

As more and more people—including you and me—operationalize love as a core business strategy, it will change the world for the better. As in the "whole wide world," as we used to say when we were kids. But we are kids no longer. We have big responsibilities.

We have an obligation to make sure that our collective future is markedly better than the present. And from what I've seen—and from what you've read in this book—we are up to the task.

And it doesn't have to be all that complicated. Because, as you now know, it's really just a matter of waking up every day and striving to do what you love in the service of people who love what you do.

Are you in?

NOTES

Chapter 1

Epigraph

C. S. Lewis, *The Four Loves*, reissue edition, originally published 1960 (New York: HarperCollins, 2017.

1. Korn Ferry, "Korn Ferry Global Study: Majority of CEOs See More Value in Technology Than Their Workforce," November 17, 2016, https://www.kornferry.com/press/korn-ferry-global-study-majority-of-ceos-see-more-value-in-technology-than-their-workforce.
2. The 2015 survey was conducted by aAdvantage Consulting, a Singapore-based firm, and the British-based Barrett Values Centre.

Chapter 2

Epigraph

I first heard this in an interview on the *Motley Fool* website. You can still watch it on YouTube: "An Interview with Warren Buffett, Part 2 of 9," September 16, 2012, accessed December 31, 2018, https://youtu.be/KCUL00-8dCo.

1. Mark J. Perry, "Why Socialism Always Fails," American Enterprise Institute (AEI), March 22, 2016, accessed August 30, 2017, http://www.aei.org/publication/why-socialism-always-fails/.
2. "Interview with John Piper," *Ask Pastor John*, desiringGod.org, July 28, 2015, accessed August 30, 2017, http://www.desiringgod.org/interviews/what-is-love.
3. C. S. Lewis, *The Four Loves*, reissue edition, originally published 1960 (New York: HarperCollins, 2017).
4. "U.S. Employee Engagement," *Gallup Daily*, accessed December 31, 2018, https://news.gallup.com/poll/180404/gallup-daily-employee-engagement.aspx.
5. *2017 Training Industry Report*, *Training* magazine, November–December 2017, accessed December 31, 2018, https://trainingmag.com/trgmag-article/2017-training-industry-report/.

6. This is the quote you saw at the start of the chapter. If you missed the note there, this interview is available on YouTube, "An Interview with Warren Buffett, Part 2 of 9," September 16, 2012, https://youtu.be/KCUL00-8dCo.
7. Chris Myers, "Why Are Millennials So Hard to Manage? The Modern Workplace Might Be to Blame," *Forbes*, July 6, 2016.

Chapter 3

Epigraph

Gordon MacKenzie, *Orbiting the Giant Hairball: A Corporate Fool's Guide to Surviving with Grace* (New York: Viking, 1998).

1. Chrissy Scivicque, contributor, "Bad Career Advice: Do What You Love and You'll Never Work a Day," *Forbes*, September 21, 2010, accessed July 24, 2017, https://www.forbes.com/sites/work-in-progress/2010/09/21/bad-career-advice-do-what-you-love-and-youll-never-work-a-day/#5dc1a2de2245.
2. Smith said this or something similar on a number of occasions. This version comes from a plaque in the courtyard at the Poynter Institute in St. Petersburg, Florida.
3. This is also sometimes attributed to Ernest Hemingway, probably because Hemingway seemed to always use curse words when he talked about writing. But Maya Angelou attributed it to Nathaniel Hawthorne in an interview published in 1990 in the *Paris Review*.
4. André Spicer and Carl Cederström, "The Research We've Ignored About Happiness at Work," *Harvard Business Review*, July 21, 2015.
5. Steve Farber, *The Radical Leap: A Personal Lesson in Extreme Leadership* (Poway, CA: Mission Boulevard Press, 2014).
6. Stephen Caldwell, "Finding Your Job Fit," *The Life@Work Journal*, vol. 1, no. 3, August 1998.
7. Ibid.

Chapter 4

Epigraph

John Burger, "'Do Ordinary Things with Extraordinary Love': The Things That Made Mother Teresa Tick," *National Catholic Register*, August 26, 2010, accessed December 27, 2018, http://www.ncregister.com/daily-news/do-ordinary-things-with-extraordinary-love.

1. Bernie Swain, *What Made Me Who I Am* (New York: Post Hill Press, 2016).
2. Werner Berger successfully made this climb in 2018.

Chapter 5

Epigraph
Matthew Arnold, "From Hymn of Empedocles."
1. Elise Mitchell, "The Leadership Journey Line: A Leader's Guide to Finding Purpose," elisemitchell.com, https://s3.us-east-2.amazonaws.com/elisemitchelldownloads/Finding+Your+Purpose+Journey+Line+eguide.pdf.
2. Ibid.
3. Bernie Swain, *What Made Me Who I Am* (New York: Post Hill Press, 2016).
4. Brené Brown, *I Thought It Was Just Me: Women Reclaiming Power and Courage in a Culture of Shame* (New York: Penguin, 2007).

Chapter 6

Epigraph
As quoted in John Marks, *Worldwide Laws of Life: 200 Eternal Spiritual Principles* (West Conshohocken, PA: Templeton Press, 1998).
1. Dan Cable, "How Humble Leadership Really Works," *Harvard Business Review*, April 23, 2018, accessed January 3, 2019, https://hbr.org/2018/04/how-humble-leadership-really-works.
2. Kirk Thompson and Matt Waller, *Purple on the Inside* (Fayetteville, AR: Epic Books/University of Arkansas Press, 2019).

Chapter 7

Epigraph
Leo Rosten, from a speech delivered at the National Book Awards in New York in 1962.
1. Lonnie Golden with J. Henly, S. Lambert, and J. Kim, "Work Schedule Flexibility for Workers: A Path to Employee Happiness?," *Journal of Social Research and Policy*, Symposium Issue: Between Wealth and Well Being, vol. 4, no. 2, December 2013, pp. 107–135.

Chapter 8

Epigraph
Ann Voskamp, *The Broken Way: A Daring Path into the Abundant Life* (Grand Rapids, MI: Zondervan, 2016).

1. Kirk Thompson and Matt Waller, *Purple on the Inside* (Fayetteville, AR: University of Arkansas Press/Epic Books, 2019).

Chapter 9

Epigraph

Simon Sinek, Twitter post on August 2, 2018, accessed December 31, 2018, https://twitter.com/simonsinek/status/1025044649726095361?lang=en.

Chapter 10

Epigraph

From the cover of John Bunyan, *The Poetry of John Bunyan*, Volume II: *You Have Not Lived Today Until You Have Done Something for Someone Who Can Never Repay You* (Portable Poetry, 2017).

Chapter 11

Epigraph

This is something Tom Peters said multiple times in conversations with me and with clients.

INDEX

ABOUT STEVE FARBER AND THE EXTREME LEADERSHIP INSTITUTE

Listed as one of *Inc.*'s global Top 50 Leadership and Management Experts, Steve Farber is a leadership pioneer, strategist, keynote speaker, and bestselling author on Extreme Leadership. His expertise is in creating organizational cultures where leadership is an opportunity and obligation not just for those in authority but for everyone at all levels.

His accessible, deeply inspirational, and eminently practical Radical LEAP framework is widely used across the business, nonprofit, and education spectrum. Steve has been credited with redefining leadership in deeply personal yet practical terms and with reenergizing thousands of people to make a significant difference in their businesses, lives, and the world around them. Steve's Extreme Leadership Institute team develops programs with one thing in mind: radical results for clients. The institute's talented consultants have helped more than 20 companies achieve "Best Place to Work" status.

Steve and The Extreme Leadership Institute team can work with you in the following ways:

- Deliver practical, inspiring, and entertaining keynote speeches to your employees and colleagues

- Operationalize love in your business to earn a competitive advantage

- Embed the practices of Extreme Leadership in your organization's DNA

- Provide significant ongoing leadership learning and development

- Create and amplify deep employee engagement

- Develop your award-winning culture

- Help you achieve radical results

Steve has worked with Johns Hopkins, Cisco, Intel, TriNet, Hyatt, and hundreds of other organizations large and small. He has spoken to or worked with corporate clients in virtually every industry there is, from the tech sector to financial services, manufacturing, healthcare, hospitality, entertainment, public education, retail, and government.

To book Steve Farber for your next event, visit www.Steve Farber.com.

To learn about The Extreme Leadership Institute's consulting, coaching, and training services, visit www.ExtremeLeadership .com.

For free (because we love you), you'll find tools and assessments to help you operationalize love in your business at www .LoveIsGoodBiz.com.